Bringing the Course to Life

How to Unlock the Meaning of *A Course in Miracles* for Yourself

by Allen Watson & Robert Perry

#24 in a series based on *A Course in Miracles*

This is the twenty-fourth book in a series, each of which deals with the modern spiritual teaching *A Course in Miracles*. If you would like to receive future publications directly from the publisher, or if you would like to receive the newsletter that accompanies this series, please write us at the address below.

The Circle of Atonement
Teaching and Healing Center
P.O. Box 4238
West Sedona, AZ 86340
(520) 282-0790, Fax (520) 282-0523
E-mail: circleofa@sedona.net
Website: http://nen.sedona.net/circleofa/

The Foundation for *A Course in Miracles* (often referred to as "FACIM"), the current holder of the copyright for *A Course in Miracles*, also holds a federal registration for the designation *"A Course in Miracles"* as a service mark and claims the exclusive right to the use of that designation in titles. A service mark identifies and distinguishes the source of the services of one party from those of others. Much confusion has resulted from the attempt by FACIM to appropriate as a service mark the designation *"A Course in Miracles,"* which is the proper name of a book. A cancellation action is pending in the United States Trademark Office which seeks the cancellation of the service mark. The Circle of Atonement and the book entitled *A Course in Miracles,* not FACIM, is the source of the information and teaching herein.

Copyright © 1999 by
The Circle of Atonement: Teaching and Healing Center
All rights reserved

ISBN 1-886602-14-X

Published by The Circle of Atonement: Teaching and Healing Center
Printed in the United States of America

Cover design: Sunshower Rose
Typesetting, Design & Layout: Karen Reider

TABLE OF CONTENTS

Chapter 1 Reading and Study are Fundamental 1
Chapter 2 The Course's Unique Style of Writing 9
Chapter 3 Guidance for the Beginning or Bewildered 33
Chapter 4 An Overview of the Techniques 45

    STEP I: OBSERVATION
Chapter 5 *Observation Techniques A-G* 51
Chapter 6 *Observation Techniques H-K* 65

    STEP II: INTERPRETATION
Chapter 7 *A. Being Context-Sensitive* 79
Chapter 8 *B. Plugging in the Meaning of Terms,*
    Phrases and Pronouns 93
Chapter 9 *C. Getting the Meaning of the Sentence* 107
Chapter 10 *D. Following the Logic* 113
Chapter 11 *E. Recognizing When Passages*
    Address Specific Situations, Issues or Beliefs 127
Chapter 12 *F. Identifying Irony and Statements of False Arguments* 141
Chapter 13 *G. Understanding and Appreciating Biblical References* 149
Chapter 14 *H. Summarizing the Message* 165

    STEP III: APPLICATION
Chapter 15 *A. Experiencing and Visualizing the Passage* 179
Chapter 16 *B. Reading the Passage as Personally Addressing You* 193
Chapter 17 *C. Identifying in Yourself Thoughts or States*
    of Mind the Course Speaks About 211
Chapter 18 *D. Applying What You Are Reading to*
    the Specifics of Your Life 221

Conclusion 235

Introduction
Allen

A few years ago, Robert and I began to realize that in our study of *A Course in Miracles* we had developed a large number of techniques that had brought the words of the Course to life in a new way for both of us. Some of these techniques were things one or the other of us had stumbled upon ourselves. In my case, many of them were things I had picked up from master students of the Bible during my years of Bible study. When put together, all of these techniques had helped us both to mine new riches from the Course.

In preparing for our Text Study classes, Robert and I were using these techniques regularly. What we were not doing, however, was imparting these tools for study to our students. We resolved that, if we were to be good teachers, we had to begin to do exactly that. And so we put together a weekend intensive on study methods, entitled, Bringing the Course to Life. We wrote down all of the techniques we could think of, found examples of how to apply them, and presented them to about twenty students in Sedona, during one long weekend.

Many of the students who attended that class have told us that it revolutionized their relationship with the Text. Perhaps for the first time for some, they had begun to feel that *they themselves* could study and really understand the Text. We have continued to see this happen as more students listen to the tapes from that intensive. The overall impact of that weekend was so great that we decided to turn the material from the intensive into a book.

Experience has convinced us that these techniques can transform how you approach the reading of the Course. There is so much more in the Course than students have guessed. There is a wealth of transformative meaning waiting to be uncovered. In this book, we attempt to show how to do that, through instruction, examples and exercises. In our examples and exercises, we go into minute detail, detail that you may find imposing. We urge you to not let this deter you. We are not suggesting that you go into Course passages in the same level of depth and detail. Some of the techniques – for instance, understanding biblical references – are ones that you may not personally find meaningful. We are simply trying to show what is possible. We are trying to show just how much meaning is in those passages. This realization alone can change the way in which one reads the Course.

We offer these techniques to you in the hope that they do for you what they have done for us – that they enable you to unlock the meaning of *A Course in Miracles* for yourself.

Chapter 1

Reading and Study are Fundamental

A Course in Miracles is a spiritual path, just as Christianity and Buddhism are. This spiritual path, however, comes to us in the form of a book, and this carries one crucial and immediate implication: The foundational activity of a student of this path is *reading the book*. There is much more to being a student of the Course, but that is where it starts. Everything else is based on that.

As an analogy, for many people, Christianity comes primarily in the form of a church. From this it follows that the foundational activity for a Christian (in this view) is going to church. There's more to being a Christian than that, but that is seen as the base, the starting-point. In both cases (the Course and Christianity), the idea is the same: If a spiritual path comes to you in a certain form, then being a follower of that path means *taking part in that form*. A Course in Miracles comes to us as a book; to be a follower of this path means that you read the book.

That is even implied by what we call followers of this path: *students*. A student, by definition, is one who studies. The word "student," in fact, comes from the Latin *studere*, to study. Unless you study, how can you be a student, how can you be "one who studies"?

This is also the clear implication of this path taking the form of an educational course. If someone says to you, "This is a course, and here is the text," what do you think you are expected to do with that text? Does anyone need to tell you that you are supposed to study it? An educational course may end up teaching you things that, by itself, its text could not. It may, for instance, teach you hands-on skills through lab work. Yet even these skills rest on the foundation of studying that course's text. And so it is with this course. Everything is based on studying the book. That is the foundation for all the rest.

Course students, oddly enough, often resist this idea. To many, it seems sufficient to attend a study group, or to soak up the Course's ideas through friends who read it, or through other books that refer to it. Many other students believe in reading the Course, but not *studying* it. Studying implies a close, detailed examination of something. It implies reading and re-reading. It implies concentration and reflection. For many students, this smacks of an impractical "head-trip" which pulls us away from the "universal experience" (C-In.2:5) to which the Course leads us.

This perspective is part of a pervasive anti-intellectual sentiment that exists among many Course students. This sentiment pits the heart (considered inherently spiritual) against the mind (considered inherently egoic). It pits feeling (the goal) against thinking (the block). The aim in this view is to get out of your mind, out of your head, and into your feelings, your heart. This is seen as synonymous with getting out of your ego and diving directly into God.

This view is so common that many students assume that it comes from the Course itself. It may come as a shock to learn that there is not a shred of this view in the Course. The Course never once elevates feeling over thinking, or heart over mind. Not only that, it never even *contrasts* the two. This may be surprising given the ideas currently circulating in alternative spiritual circles, but the Course never once contrasts thinking and feeling, or mind and heart. Not once.

The role of study

Instead, the Course reverses some of the prevailing views about the relationship between the intellect and spirituality. The intellect is often seen as the enemy of spiritual awakening. Yet, in the Course's view, an intellectual activity like study is not a block to spiritual experience. It is the *gateway*. It is the foundation. We see this clearly in the opening lines of the Workbook:

> A theoretical foundation such as the text provides is necessary as a framework to make the exercises in this workbook meaningful.

This says it with unmistakable clarity. The Text is the foundation for the Workbook. Theory is the foundation for practice. The Text's theory is actually *necessary* to make the Workbook exercises meaningful. Without that theory, the exercises will be deprived of meaning. This is how many students feel who pick up the Workbook without studying the Text first. They wonder, "What on earth do these lessons mean?"

Studying the Text enables us to make sense out of the Workbook exercises. And the Workbook exercises carry us into experience. Study, therefore, is the foundation for experience.

We are told the same thing early in the Text (see T-1.VII.4-5). There, it says that when the Course finally leads us to the direct experience of God, we can experience it as beatific or as traumatic. It can seem to be a holy experience of awe or a terrifying experience of fear. What decides which way it will be for us? Whether or not we have laid a solid foundation through study (T-1.VII.4:3-4, 5:8). Once we come face-to-face with God, our study is not suddenly rendered irrelevant. Rather, our study becomes the foundation for how we "instinctively" react in that moment. It determines whether we are able to fearlessly unite with God, or whether we recoil in terror. That is how important study is.

How can this be? How can study be such a powerful force on the spiritual path? To appreciate this, we must understand how the Course sees the spiritual journey. The fundamental problem, as the Course sees it, is our perception. Our perception is the root of our suffering because our perception determines our emotion. If we *perceive* that someone wants to hurt us and has the power to do so, we will *feel* afraid. If we *perceive* an action of ours as destructive, insensitive, and cruel, we will *feel* guilty. If we *perceive* a person as attractive and desirable, as someone we want to join with, we will *feel* love.

Our perceptions, then, determine our emotional experience. Yet what are perceptions? They are our interpretations of what things mean. Our eyes show us only forms, and forms by themselves cannot produce an emotional reaction. One more step is required. Our minds have to interpret what those forms mean. If someone slaps you on the face, you can have several different emotional reactions, depending on what you decide the slap meant. You may decide the slap was an angry assault, or that it was punishment you deserved, or that it was some kind of kinky love play. Maybe the two of you are actors on a stage and the slap was in the script. Your emotional reaction in each of these situations would be different, because you would interpret the meaning of the slap differently. You would *perceive* it differently. Again, perception determines emotion.

The Course claims that what is causing our suffering is not the world, but our perception of the world. It claims that we can choose different perceptions of the same situations that seem to be causing us pain; and that when we do, our emotional state can go from agony to ecstasy, even when the outer situations remain the same.

To help us make this choice, however, the Course needs to school us. It needs to school us in the content of our current perceptions and the content of the new perceptions. Content is meaning. What are the meanings we are currently seeing in the world, the meanings that are causing us pain? What are the meanings we *could* see in the world, the meanings that could lift us beyond pain?

With this schooling, we will be able to choose the new over the old. We can remain stuck in an old perception for years, for decades, but when we suddenly see that what seemed to feel so good is causing us pain, and that another way of perceiving can cause us joy, we can finally say goodbye to that old perception. For instance, we may have been convinced our entire lives that seeing ourselves as special feels good. But when we learn that specialness brings guilt (since it elevates ourselves at the expense of others) and loneliness (since it singles us out as unique and thus sets us apart from others), we may decide we no longer want that perception. And when we are shown that seeing others as our equals brings happiness, we may decide to choose that perception over specialness.

This is the purpose of studying the Course. Through study we acquire the learning that makes a new choice possible. Now we are ready to practice making that new choice. This is where the Workbook comes in. It teaches us the practice. But this practice is not going to make much sense unless we have laid a good foundation of study. Most Workbook practice is simply the repetition of different sentences. The words themselves, however, are not the agent of change. It is the meaning of those words. The meaning is what we are really practicing when we repeat a lesson, a thought for the day. That meaning can carry our minds to new places. It can lift us out of painful emotions into peace. But in order for it to do that, we have to *see* the meaning in the sentence. And that comes from study. If all we have are the words of a lesson and our basic grasp of English, those words will mean a fraction of what they could have meant, and will often convey incorrect meanings to our minds. Yet with a solid background of study, those same words will carry a wealth of profound meaning. They will have the power to move our minds out of the most entrenched emotional pain. One of the things our students in Sedona have said to us time and again is how much more powerful their Workbook practice has become as a result of deep study of the Text.

For these reasons, studying the Course is quite a different enterprise from studying other books, even most other spiritual books. For the Course is interested only in those ideas that contain transformative meaning, meaning that is the very substance of new perception, meaning that has the power to reverse our dejected emotional state. This meaning can even carry us beyond what we normally call emotion into spiritual states. The Course's ideas are therefore extremely practical. From our standpoint, they are the most practical things in the world.

This also means that the Course intentionally avoids ideas that do not directly shift perception. It refuses to take a stand on reincarnation (see M-24); it never discusses chakras, astral planes, diet, exercise, ancient civilizations, or future prophecies. It carefully avoids those ideas that are often associated with spirituality, yet which, once taken into our minds, leave those minds in the same basic state they were before. When you truly take the Course's ideas into your mind, your mind is changed, your mental state is transfigured. These ideas are not just irrelevant theory. They are the stuff of salvation.

And that is why we study.

The need to read in a new way

The need for reading and study would not be something we resist so much if the Course's language was easier to understand. Yet the universal reaction of Course students is that the language is exceedingly difficult. In discussing the topic of the Course being translated into other languages, we have more than once heard someone ask when it is going to be translated into *English!*

That, of course, is why we have written this book. Our conviction is that the Course is written in a unique way and was written in this way for a purpose. We, therefore, must approach the reading of the Course in a new way. We must bring our whole mind to the act of reading and read in a way that harmonizes with the Course's unique style. We must learn a new style of reading. Only then can the Course's new style of writing do the work in us it was intended to do.

While the bulk of this book will be about how to read and study the Course, before we can get into that we need to lay more foundation. We need to explore the Course's unique style of writing. That is the subject of the next chapter.

Chapter 2

The Course's Unique Style of Writing

As soon as we try to study the Text, we face a major problem: the Text is not written like anything else in the world. It has a style all its own, a style that disregards some of our culture's most basic writing conventions. This style can seem maddening at times, yet we will see in this chapter that there is a definite method to its "madness."

Ideally, any attempt to fruitfully study the Text should be in harmony with this unique style. Thus, before we can establish a method for studying the Text – which is the aim of this book – we must gain some sense of the style in which it is written. We will examine three different aspects of this unique style below.

1. Symphonic and holographic rather than linear

A standard textbook is written in a linear fashion. This means that it begins with the more simple and foundational ideas and builds to more complex and sophisticated ideas. This also means that it follows a single train of thought at any given moment.

The Course's style is dramatically different. As first pointed out by Ken Wapnick, the Course is written *symphonically*. Like a symphony, the Course introduces themes, sets them aside, then reintroduces them, explores and develops them, and interweaves them with other themes. In any given section in the Course, literally dozens of themes might be active,[1] interweaving with each other in a dizzying profusion of meaning.

Before we explore the rich benefits of this symphonic style, we must acknowledge that this style can easily frustrate and confuse the reader. Because of the many interweaving themes, the Text can *appear* to be a garbled, meandering train of disconnected ideas, a train which has no tracks and so wanders aimlessly and randomly about, and which goes around in endless circles, repeating itself over and over. The result is that reading the Text can be a mind-numbing, sleep-inducing experience. Course students will often report that after reading several pages they have not remembered a single thing they have read. More than one student has asked in bewilderment and frustration, "Why is the Course written in this infernal convoluted way?!"

For many years that question lingered in the back of my mind. I (the first-person remarks in this chapter are Robert's)

---

[1] We come up with this rather large number based on considering a repeating key term (such as "dream," or "healing") to be a theme. A given section will have dozens of such repeating terms, each one representing a specific world of thought, one that is often somewhat specific to that section and surrounding ones. One could count the number of themes instead by counting the composite themes developed using those key terms. This would yield a minimum of half a dozen to perhaps a dozen themes per section.

had this nagging suspicion that, had the Course been written differently, it would have been far more effective. I thought that it was *less* integrated than ordinary writing, by which I mean that a word, sentence or idea seemed to have only a tenuous connection with what came before and after it. The writing rambled more, said things for no apparent reason, was filled with extraneous material and jumped from one sentence to the next without much rhyme or reason – or so it appeared. In fact, my goal as an interpreter seemed to be to dig out the ideas buried in this tangled verbiage and restate them – this time clearly and plainly. This idea, however, aroused a vague mental discomfort, for my plan definitely implied that my restatement of the Course would be more useful than the Course itself. This did not reflect well on my spiritual path.

However, over the years I slowly realized that I could not have been more mistaken about the Course's writing. I saw that my initial reactions were analogous to the reactions of a dog as he watched a master chef fixing a gourmet meal in the kitchen. That dog would see a series of confusing actions that would seem randomly strung together without reason. He would not understand that he was watching an orchestrated activity leading to a purposeful end. I slowly came to see that the Course's writing also was a highly orchestrated activity; so highly orchestrated, in fact, that the mind of the author appeared to tower above mine, as a chef's mind surpasses that of a dog.

Eventually, I came to see that the Course's writing is far *more* integrated than ordinary writing, rather than less. I saw that each sentence always connected meaningfully with what came before it, and that often this unverbalized connection added a wealth of new meaning. Further, I began to notice that numerous lines of connection reached out from each sentence, linking it not only with the sentences directly before and after it, but also with sentences in the surrounding pages, in other chapters, and sometimes hundreds of pages away. I saw that each section does not just develop a single theme, but weaves together a myriad of themes, revealing multiple relationships between them. Rather than being verbose and padded, the Course, I realized, is a rich and meaningful tapestry whose every word and idea fits smoothly into the larger pattern. Instead of being disjointed and rambling, the Course's sentences and paragraphs actually form a dense web of rich interconnectedness.

What does this interconnectedness look like? Something from a previous passage shows up in a later passage. A key word, a phrase, an image or a specific idea from a previous passage appears again in the passage we are currently reading. To demonstrate how this works I will use Paragraph 8 from "The Witnesses to Sin" (T-27.VI), identifying the connections in each sentence:

1. The resurrection of the world awaits your healing and your happiness, that you may demonstrate the healing of the world.

- "The resurrection of the world awaits your healing": The idea that the rebirth of a dying world awaits your healing is discussed in the previous section (T-27.V.5-7).
- "Healing": The theme of healing runs throughout this chapter, which is entitled "The Healing of the Dream."
- "That you may demonstrate": The power of a witness to

"demonstrate" or prove something is a running theme in several sections in this chapter (including I, II, V and VI). There, we learn that your health is a witness that demonstrates the world's right to be healed – the exact idea we find here.

2. The holy instant will replace all sin if you but carry its effects with you.

- "The holy instant": Entering the holy instant is a theme in the previous three sections (T-27.III, IV, V).
- "The holy instant will replace all sin [in the world]": Allowing the holy instant to shine through you and heal the damage done to the world by sin, is discussed in the previous section (T-27.V).
- "Replace all sin": Replacing sin (specifically, the *witnesses* to sin) is a theme of this current section: "For all sin's witnesses do His [the Holy Spirit's] replace" (4:9).

3. And no one will elect to suffer more.

- "No one will elect to suffer more": The idea that when you make visible your healing others will stop electing to suffer is mentioned four sections before this: "Show him your healing, and he will consent no more to suffer" (T-27.II.8:7).

4. What better function could you serve than this?

- "Function": The idea of function is discussed in two recent sections (T-27.I, II). Section I says the function you chose was that of showing your damaged body to your brother, as proof that he sinned against you and deserves to be punished. It says your *true* function is to show him your *healing*, which demonstrates that he never sinned, and that he deserves to be healed. This is the same idea we find here.

The function that you serve (in this sentence) is demonstrating or showing your healing to the world (from Sentence 1 above).

5. Be healed that you may heal, and suffer not the laws of sin to be applied to you.

- "Be healed that you may heal": This is similar to the first line of the previous section: "The only way to heal is to be healed" (T-27.V.1:1).
- "Suffer not the laws of sin to be applied to you": This section contains a discussion about the "different sufferings" (T-27.VI.6:5) that result when you think the laws of sin apply to you.

6. And truth will be revealed to you who chose to let love's symbols take the place of sin.

- "Truth will be revealed [by] love's symbols": A running theme in this chapter is that of witnesses or symbols that either reveal truth or reinforce illusion. Witnesses to truth were just discussed in Paragraph 3 of this section.
- "Let love's symbols take the place of sin": Letting love's symbols take the place of sin was discussed in Paragraphs 5 and 6 of this section.
- "Love's symbols": A recent section, "Beyond All Symbols" (T-27.III), focuses on symbols of truth, which in the Course is synonymous with symbols of love.

We have seen that these few sentences pull together a multitude of themes from this section and five previous sections, weaving these themes into a single whole. Perhaps you feel that our examples of this interweaving are forced, or obscure, something only a complete Course wizard, versed in every detail, would spot or benefit from. But it does not take a Course expert to spot such connections. In Chapter 7 we will discuss how anyone can spot more of them. Noticing *more* connections is what matters, not noticing *all* of them. Indeed, we have become convinced that noticing them all is impossible. Anyone can develop a reading habit of watching for such connections. For those who do, generous benefits will follow. And even when you don't notice the connections, you may still be affected by them, though you won't know why. Below, we attempt to categorize the benefits of the Course's symphonic style:

1. The themes grow richer and sink in deeper as they repeat.

Basic to this symphonic style is that themes repeat again and again. Yet it is not mere repetition, which would get rather tedious. Instead, each time a theme arises anew, it is discussed in connection with a new set of related themes. This draws out new dimensions of meaning in that theme. For instance, as we see how the idea of forgiveness relates to time, to the body, to the holy instant, to the miracle, to special relationships, and so on, we understand forgiveness with ever-greater depth. With each repetition, the theme expands in clarity, breadth and magnitude, allowing it to penetrate deeper into our minds. This in turn gently prepares us for the next repetition, which will draw us yet deeper into the theme, a depth for which we may not have been ready the last time around. Thus, with each turn of the spiral, we are drawn ever closer to the center of the idea, at which lies a vast wealth of meaning. And at the same time *that* spiral is turning, our minds are following scores of other spirals inward to the center of scores of other ideas. Our minds are thus progressively drawn closer and closer to the place where all of these themes meet: the unified heart of the Course's thought system.

2. The interweaving enriches both the specific passages and the larger discussions that it involves.

This interweaving makes for discussions that are saturated with meaning. It does so in at least three ways: First, when an earlier discussion is referenced in a later passage, all of the meaning of that discussion is pulled into the current passage, making it far more meaningful. Second, the previous passage also takes on more meaning and clarity; the interweaving may answer questions raised by the earlier passage. Third, these links make the Course's overall discussion more whole and unified, thus making it a more powerful reading experience. A series of dazzling but disconnected truths is not as meaningful as a network of deeply interconnected truths.

The first of these three benefits – that the current passage is enriched in meaning by pulling in the meaning of the previous passage – is perhaps the most dramatic. For an example, consider this sentence from "Choose Once Again" (T-31.VIII):

> Let us be glad that we can walk the world, and find so many chances to perceive another situation where God's gift can once again be recognized as ours! (9:1)

This sentence may sound somewhat nondescript and dull, making one wonder why the author awarded it an exclamation point. "Another boring, wordy sentence from the Course," we might mutter to ourselves. Yet this one sentence contains a plethora of references to preceding paragraphs, references that must be recognized to see the sentence's full meaning.

Taken by itself, the phrase "so many chances to perceive another situation" sounds vague and rather dry. It actually refers to this section's teaching about difficult situations. Difficult situations, we are told, "are but lessons that you failed to learn presented once again" (3:1). Presenting them once again gives us "another chance to choose again" (4:2) (notice that both "another" and "chance" occur in this sentence and in the sentence we are discussing). This idea is beautifully expressed in the image of Christ appearing to us (an image which occurs twice in this section): "In every difficulty, all distress, and each perplexity Christ calls to you and gently says, 'My brother, choose again'" (3:2).

"Let us be glad" now takes on a whole new meaning. It means, "Let us be glad about being faced with an apparently painful situation, because it gives us an opportunity for change." In fact, "let us be glad" has just been used in this exact same sense a few sections before: "Let us be glad that you will see what you believe [which means seeing a world of sin and death], [so that you can] change what you believe" (T-31.III.6:1).

The phrase "God's gift" also sounds rather vague. The previous paragraph holds the key. It told us that His gift is the vision of "a different world, so new and clean and fresh..." (8:4). In truth, God has already given us this gift, which means we need only recognize it as ours. This explains the phrase "recognized as ours" in our sentence. This paragraph also explains *how* we recognize it as ours: "To give this gift [to others] is how to make it yours" (8:6).

The gift idea also shows up two paragraphs earlier. There we are asked to give Jesus "the little gift" (7:1) of choosing again. In exchange for this gift we will receive another of God's gifts: the infinite gift of "the peace of God" (7:1). This same passage also refers to giving God's gift to others. It says that we will be given power to bring God's peace to everyone who "wanders in the world uncertain, lonely, and in constant fear" (7:1). "Wanders in the world" clearly links with the phrase "walk the world" in our sentence.

Finally, the phrase "once again" has occurred three times before in this section. The idea is that no matter how many times we have chosen wrongly and failed to learn the lesson, it will be "presented once again," so that we can "choose once again." This time we hopefully will choose correctly and thereby learn the lesson that has always stood patiently before us.

Now let us pull all of this meaning into our original sentence and see what we get:

> Let us be glad that we can walk the world and see so many people wandering alone and afraid, and experience so many difficult, distressing and trying situations! For we can perceive these difficulties as wonderful opportunities for recognizing that God's gift is ours. In these trials, the lessons we failed to learn before are presented once again, giving us yet another chance to learn. In them, Christ appears to us in all His glory, asking us to choose once again. If we choose rightly, we will learn the lesson at last and thus escape all the pain caused by our previous choices.
>
> Now that we have chosen differently, we will take our place among the saviors of the world. We will be given a vision of a new and different world, and imbued with power to bring this vision to all those wandering, hurt-

ing people. We should be glad that we can give them this vision and set their minds at peace. For only in giving God's gifts to them do we realize His gifts belong to us. And God Himself ordained that they be for us.

In the end, in exchange for our little gift of choosing again, we will recognize as ours the infinite gift of the peace of God. Let us be glad!

This sentence, which at first seemed lackluster, is now revealed to contain a wealth of meaning, meaning that is both challenging and uplifting. This is not meaning that we just arbitrarily stuck in this sentence. It is the meaning specifically revealed by this sentence's subtle allusions to previous passages. Because of those allusions, we know that something like the above was in the author's mind while he was dictating this sentence.

This exercise, hopefully, has enabled us to concretely see how the Course's interweaving works, and how powerful it is. Each time our sentence alluded to another passage, the meaning of that previous passage, like water from a pitcher, poured into our sentence. Since there were many such allusions, there were many pitchers emptying into our sentence all at once. As a result, it was immensely filled out and enriched, becoming more profound, more clear, more impactful.

Now realize that the previous passages that this sentence referred to themselves contain references to yet other passages. If we were to pull the meaning from these other passages into our sentence, think how much fuller it would grow then. And, of course, these other passages contain even further references to yet other passages. And on and on it goes. The net effect is that the entire Course is like a system of tributaries, which dumps all of its water into the ocean of the single sentence we just examined. The meaning of that sentence is truly vast, if we see it for what it is. That one sentence contains the meaning of the entire Course. And this same thing is happening, to one degree or another, with every sentence in the Course.

3. The interweaving shows how one idea connects to others, revealing the wholeness of the system and how the entire system is contained in each idea.

As we just saw, one of the main effects of the Course's symphonic style is that the whole is subtly infused into each part. Just as this happens with individual passages, so this happens with the Course's *ideas*. When one idea is discussed in connection with another, you can see that the first idea implies the second. For instance, if you deeply grasped the Course's concept of forgiveness, you would see that it implies the unreality of the body, and the unity of minds, and the ego's fixation on the past, and so on. To say that forgiveness implies these ideas is to say that it *contains* them. For they are all *part* of the concept of forgiveness. And since forgiveness implies all of the ideas in the Course, it contains all of them. Inside the single idea of forgiveness is contained the Course's entire thought system. And this is true of *every* idea in the Course. Every one implicitly contains the whole system.

In addition to being symphonic, then, we like to call the Course's style of writing *holographic.* (We are indebted to a member of Allen Watson's New Jersey study group for the use of this word.) In the Course, just as in a hologram, each part contains the whole. The Workbook, in fact, explicitly claims this holographic quality for its daily thoughts (most of which are brief, ten-syllable sentences). "Each contains the whole curriculum" (W-pI.rVI.IN.2:2). As we attempted to show in the preceding two points, this holographic style yields a course in which each passage and each idea is soaked with layer upon layer, web upon web of meaning; in which the boundless meaning of the whole is poured like wine into each and every part.

You can imagine what this holographic and symphonic style can do to one's reading experience, if one truly appreciates it. Each section and indeed each paragraph becomes a true symphony of meaning. As one notices more and more of the connections between passages, one realizes that each sentence is glowing with an unexpected fullness of meaning. As one also sees new connections between ideas, new and unexpected links are formed in the mind. Meanwhile, new elements, new themes, are constantly being gathered into the music. Thus, the Course's symphony grows richer with each passing page. And as this symphony expands and deepens, so does the reader's mind expand and deepen with it. As larger and larger tapestries of connection emerge, one eventually realizes that the meaning disclosed is literally inexhaustible; that at bottom it opens out into a numinous sense beyond the expressible, into transcendental intimations beyond the edge of conceptual thought. The mind has been led to the gates of the eternal through the reading of a book.

2. Seeks to transform rather than just inform

A conventional textbook attempts to inform and instruct, to teach a body of ideas. The Course's Text attempts this also. Throughout, the Text is trying to teach us a sophisticated system of ideas. Yet the author of the Course does not just want to teach our intellects a set of concepts. He wants those concepts to go in so deeply that they transform our fundamental mental/emotional outlook. He wants to move our minds, to sway our most basic posture towards reality. He wants to sell us on a new orientation towards everything. This is his idea of "teaching."

We already saw hints of this in the previous point. The Course's symphonic writing style means that it is not just a straight presentation of ideas. It is also a work of art. And art is designed to stir people, to affect them on levels deeper than the intellect. In the Course's hands, art becomes a tool to move the minds of its students toward a new stance toward reality.

Even the design of the Course's thought system betrays this artistic element, for its abstract and lofty system is not constructed of dry, lifeless terms, but of *characters* moving through *places* and *events*. We have the characters of God, the ego, the Holy Spirit and "you" – the reader. We read of places such as Heaven, the real world, the lawns before the gate of Heaven and the borderland. There are visual images such as the face of Christ, the Great Rays, shadow figures, thorns and lilies; auditory images like the Word of God and the Song of Heaven; and events such as the separation, the tiny tick and the final step.

This artistic element is further enhanced by the fact that much of the Course is written in iambic pentameter, Shakespearean blank verse. In iambic pentameter each line consists of ten syllables. These are broken up into five "feet" of two syllables each, with the accent on the second syllable of each foot. For example, "I *will* • not *fear* • to *look* • with*in* • to*day*" (Workbook Lesson 309). This adds a lovely cadence to the writing and increases the feeling that (as one student put it) the Course is singing to you. Iambic pentameter begins in Chapter 24 of the Text and continues through the end of the Text in Chapter 31. It then begins in Lesson 98 of the Workbook and continues unbroken for the remainder of the Workbook.

Because the author wants to transform rather than merely inform, his writing performs a much broader range of functions than that of a normal textbook. He seeks to move our minds in every way possible. He pulls every string he can find. He does adopt the guise of a professor, but he also sounds at different times like a therapist, a coach, a poet, a salesman, a friend, a spiritual master and an older brother. The following is a partial list of the many functions the Course's author seeks to fulfill through his writing:

He tries to convince and persuade, often by using logical arguments: "*Only perfect love exists. If there is fear, it produces a state that does not exist*" (T-1.VI.5:7-8).

He makes emotional appeals: "O my brothers, if you only knew the peace that will envelop you and hold you safe and pure and lovely in the Mind of God, you could but rush to meet Him where His altar is" (C-4.8:1).

He makes promises: "Believe this and you will be free" (T-1.VI.5:9).

He gives encouragement and confidence: "Go on; clouds cannot stop you....You cannot fail because your will is His" (W-pI.69.6:5,7:4).

He comforts: "How can you who are so holy suffer? All your past except its beauty is gone, and nothing is left but a blessing" (T-5.IV.8:1-2).

He blesses us: "How blessed are you who let this gift be given!" (T-22.VI.5:4). "My peace I give you" (T-13.VII.16:8).

He implores us: "My brothers in salvation, do not fail to hear my voice and listen to my words. I ask for nothing but your own release" (T-31.VIII.8:1-2). "O let your patient in, for he has come to you from God" (P-2.VII.9:9).

He breaks into celebration: "The peace of God descends on all the world, and we can see. And we can see!" (M-19.5:12-13).

He sometimes prays directly to God: "I thank You, Father, for these holy ones who are my brothers as they are Your Sons" (T-31.VIII.10:1).

He often lapses into sheer poetry: "Where stood a cross stands now the risen Christ, and ancient scars are healed within His sight" (T-26.IX.8:4).

He uses striking images, both beautiful and grotesque: "The room becomes a temple, and the street a stream of stars that brushes lightly past all sickly dreams" (P-2.VII.8:4). "Can you paint rosy lips upon a skeleton, dress it in loveliness, pet it and pamper it, and make it live?" (T-23.II.18:8).

He asks confrontive rhetorical questions: "And can you be content with an illusion that you are living?" (This line directly follows the above quote about making a skeleton live.)

He instructs us to stop and reflect on what he is saying: "Pause and reflect on this" (W-pI.155.12:2). "Think but an instant on this: God gave the Sonship to you, to ensure your perfect creation" (T-15.VIII.4:1).

He exhorts us: "Believe not that you cannot teach His perfect peace. Stand not outside, but join with me within. Fail not the only purpose to which my teaching calls you. Restore to God His Son as He created him, by teaching him his innocence" (T-14.V.9:7-10).

He gives us direct injunctions to apply his message: "Free your brother here, as I freed you" (T-19.IV(D).18:1). "Forgive your brother all appearances, that are but ancient lessons you have taught yourself about the sinfulness in you" (T-31.II.9:1).

Throughout the Course, he addresses us directly and personally: "To you who seem to find this course to be too difficult to learn..." (T-31.IV.7:3). "You who perceive yourself as weak and frail, with futile hopes and devastated dreams, born but to die, to weep and suffer pain, hear this..." (W-pI.191.9:1). Sometimes he addresses us as "brother," at other times "child": "Brother, there is no death" (T-27.II.6:8). "They are but toys, my child, so do not grieve for them" (T-30.IV.4:6).

He speaks to us so personally that he seems to be inside our minds, privy to our most private thoughts, our inmost fears and conceits, and our guilty secrets. "Look fairly at whatever makes you give your brother only partial welcome....Is it not always your belief your specialness is limited by your relationship?" (T-24.I.7:8-9).

And in complete contrast to a normal author, the Course's author occasionally speaks about his relationship with the reader: "My faith in you is as strong as all the love I give my Father. My trust in you is without limit, and without the fear that you will hear me not" (T-13.X.13:4-5). "And I will join you there, as long ago I promised and promise still" (T-19.IV(A).16:4).

This is all happening while the Text is performing its role as a textbook. While the Text is explaining to us its system of ideas, it is also attempting to *move* us. And this can obscure, at least at first, the clarity of its explanations. Yet even though some initial clarity is lost, so much more is gained.

3. Fills familiar terms with new meaning

There is yet another way in which the Course's style differs from conventional writing: its use of terms. Normally, authors choose their terms according to two usual methods. One method, of course, is to use familiar terms to communicate familiar meaning. Using time-honored terms allows others to readily understand what you mean. It also allows them to situate your message in a particular context, a context which will hopefully lend credibility to your message. For instance, using Christian terms allows your message to rest on whatever authority Christianity has with your audience. If it has no such authority, you had best not use its terms.

The other method is the direct opposite. If you have a *new* idea you will want to invent a new term for it. This stamps your idea as something truly novel, setting it apart from what has gone before. And if your new term is a catchy one, it can be an effective vehicle for helping your new idea catch on.

The Course has taken a third road, one that is drastically different from the above two. The Course wants to express new meanings. But it refuses to invent new words (though it does invent a number of new terms by combining words; e.g., "holy instant" and "special relationship"). Instead, it expresses its new meaning by using familiar terms, often ancient terms laden with centuries of tradition, connotation and nuance.

There is some root or essential meaning the Course wants to take advantage of in these terms. Being part of our culture, these terms are like ancient roads that lead our minds to a certain destination. Christian terms, for instance, are roadways that lead our minds in the direction of the Divine. They call to mind the Divine. Were the Course to invent a new term, say, for God – if it were to call God "Dopar" – this symbol wouldn't have nearly the psychological potency as the word "God." It wouldn't have those well-worn grooves inside our minds that carry us from the term to its meaning, from the *word* "God" to the *concept* of God.

Yet, while the Course wants to take advantage of these terms, it also disapproves of significant aspects of their traditional meaning. In the Course's eyes, these roads have consistently carried our minds to the wrong destination. They have called to mind a false concept of the Divine, the very concept the Course wants to correct.

The Course's solution is to use a familiar term, but fill it with a new meaning. The Course, therefore, keeps some basic meaning of a term – for it wants to take advantage of the term's ability to call this basic meaning to mind. Yet, without explanation, the Course will gut the rest of the term and infuse it with a dramatically different meaning.

This filling of familiar forms with new meaning and purpose is a favorite device of the Course. This, after all, is exactly what it has done with the idea of a *course*. It has borrowed the form of an educational course, with text, workbook and teacher's manual, and then used it to do what no standard course would do: teach us *miracles* and awaken us to God. By using this device, the Course's design is mirroring its own teaching. For this is exactly what it teaches us that the Holy Spirit does. According to the Course, the Holy Spirit takes all the forms and abilities we made, and gives them a new purpose and meaning.

Bringing the Course to Life

Giving familiar words a new meaning, however, produces a very confusing situation for the reader. This method has confounded everyone who has picked up *A Course in Miracles*. We see a familiar term on the page and expect it to carry its traditional meaning. We see the word "Christ" and expect it to refer to Jesus of Nazareth as God's only begotten Son. We see the word "miracle" and assume that it refers to the magical transformation of sick bodies and difficult situations.

The Course's terminology not only produces confusion, but also anger and aversion. Many who have left traditional Christianity read the Course's Christian terms and are turned off. Feminists read the Course's masculine terms and conclude that the Course is sexist. Christians read familiar terms and are at first drawn in, but then are repulsed when they sense a decidedly non-traditional meaning.

Why, then, did the author adopt this method, when it was sure to cause rampant confusion and bad feelings? Was it simply a bad idea? The truth, we believe, is that this method actually carries a powerful positive effect, which makes it worth all the turmoil it causes.

For example, by using the familiar term, "Son of God," the Course taps into the complex and emotionally-laden world of meaning, lodged deep in our minds, around that term. The Course likes this term's traditional connotation of someone who shares an intimate closeness with God, someone whom God looks upon as a father looks on a son, someone who is the extension of God's Own Identity and the heir to all that God has. This term has the ability to carry our minds to this particular realm of meaning, and the Course wants to make use of that ability.

Yet the Course deeply disapproves of the traditional meaning, which says that this someone is *someone besides us*. Traditionally, of course, "Son of God" refers to the idea that God has only one begotten Son: Jesus Christ. This leaves us feeling cast outside the inner circle of God's Love. Simply by using the term "Son of God," the Course accesses this feeling of not being fully included or fully embraced by God.

This, however, is not the meaning the Course sees in the term. Instead, it has filled the term with new meaning. While retaining the idea that *someone* is the apple of God's eye, it has added that this someone is *us*. We are God's Son. We share a closeness with Him that, like a blood tie, is thicker than anything that can happen in this world. We are cherished by Him as a father cherishes a son. We are a chip off of His old block. We are the heir to all that is His.

What happens, then, when the Course uses this term? Initially, the term does just what it used to do. It calls to mind the idea that someone is intimately included in God's Heart, and that someone is Jesus. Slowly, however, we become aware that the term means something different in the Course. It means that this someone is us, that we are just as included by God as we always thought that Jesus was.

For a time, when the term is used, both meanings come to mind. The old meaning is accessed and directly encounters the new meaning. Darkness and light meet face to face. The result is that each time we come across the term in the Course, a little of the old meaning gets shined away, to be replaced by the new. For the new meaning simply feels more attractive, compelling and true; and the Course uses the term so repeatedly and with such certainty that its new meaning is all the term *really* means. Eventually, a complete replacement occurs. Now when the term carries our mind to the idea that there is someone who is innately close to God, instead of seeing someone else there, we will see ourselves. Every time we hear the term "Son of God," we will be reminded how completely God has included us, how permanently and absolutely He has embraced us. At this point, the Course has erased the old meaning and healed the painful emotions associated with it. Not only that, even the term that triggered that meaning and emotion has been absorbed into the new system. Now that term only triggers the new meaning. All trace of the old meaning has vanished.

With many terms the Course does something slightly different. In these cases, the Course takes the term's meaning and simply deepens and broadens it. The term thus becomes a comprehensive teaching about life. For instance, by "insanity," we normally mean a break with socially-constructed reality and a retreat into a private world. The Course expands this concept into metaphysical proportions. It means by "insanity" a break with *divine* reality and a retreat into a separate mind; a break with transcendental oneness and a retreat into separate selfhood. This has dramatic implications, as can be seen in this passage:

> [Being] unsure of what you really are [i.e., the Son of God]...is the depth of madness. Yet it ["Who am I?"] is the universal question of the world. What does this mean except the world is mad? Why share its madness in the sad belief that what is universal here is true?
> (W-pI.139.6:2-5)

This new definition of insanity means that everything in

the physical universe is insane; that the universe itself is the very picture of insanity. As we slowly associate this new meaning with the word "insanity," our perception of our world changes. Before, we assumed that what is universally agreed upon in this world must be true. Indeed, breaking with the social consensus was the *definition* of insanity. This kept us tied to that consensus, out of fear of being labelled insane. Now, we begin to consider that the consensus itself might be insane. We entertain the possibility that someone who becomes truly sane here might look mad from the world's perspective.

Just as with the term "Son of God," the Course has retained the term's core meaning while correcting other aspects of it. It has retained the idea that insanity is a retreat from reality, yet it has shifted the meaning of "reality" from social consensus to transcendental oneness.

Reading the Course, then, involves learning a new language. This is very different from learning a foreign language. For a foreign language uses different words to express what is essentially the same world of meaning – the *egoic* world of meaning. In contrast, the Course uses the *same* words to express a *different* world of meaning, meaning that is *ego-dispelling*. The ideas in this new world frequently have no English equivalent, and often no equivalent in *any* language. For this reason, a few Course glossaries and dictionaries have been published, among which is my *A Course Glossary: 158 Definitions from "A Course in Miracles."*

Learning this new language, though difficult, is genuinely worth it. As our words become slowly cleansed of their old egoic meaning and filled with a new ego-dispelling meaning, this also happens in our minds. The dark meaning that has kept us bound is pushed out of the house of our minds, just as it was pushed out of our words, and replaced with pure light. And that is the goal of *A Course in Miracles*.

Conclusion

The Course's style does make for difficult reading, especially at first. Each of the three elements of style that we examined in this chapter get in the way of a straightforward presentation of concepts. Yet we discovered that each one was not just a case of poor and careless writing, but had a carefully planned purpose. All of the methods we explored are designed to give the Course's words and ideas greater transformative impact on our thinking, greater ability to enter and deeply affect our minds. So complete is the author's focus on this one thing that he is willing to risk the initial boredom, confusion and ire of his readers, if in the end he can turn their minds right-side up again. In his single-minded drive to liberate our minds he has developed an original style that is a unique tool of mind change.

That this intent to change our minds is embodied in the Course's writing means one very important thing: *Just reading the Course is transformative* – that is, *if* one's reading is in harmony with its style, rather than confounded by that style. The rest of this book will discuss how to read the Course. The techniques we will explore are specifically tailored to fit the Course's strange and confounding, but ultimately profound and transformative style.

Chapter 3

Guidance for the Beginning or Bewildered

Perhaps you are just beginning to study the Text for the first time. Perhaps you have made numerous attempts to read it, without much success. Perhaps you have read bits and pieces here and there, and feel as though you have probably read most of it, but you have never made a systematic study of it and do not have a clear overall grasp of its content. If you fit any of these categories, you probably feel a bit intimidated and daunted by the Text. You may even feel bewildered by it; the Text can be confusing, particularly if you have not learned how to read analytically. Its style, as we saw in the last chapter, takes considerable getting used to. Its sometimes archaic way of phrasing things seems impenetrable.

Besides the archaic language and intricate, interwoven style, the thought system being presented is so contrary to the way we have all learned to think that our minds have a hard time absorbing the thoughts:

> Simplicity is very difficult for twisted minds....Nothing is so alien to you as the simple truth, and nothing are you less inclined to listen to. (T-14.II.2:3,5)

For these reasons, we think it may be helpful to offer you some simple advice on how to get started reading this intimidating book.

Our first bit of advice is to suggest reading another book: *How To Read A Book*, by Mortimer Adler and Charles Van Doren. I (the first-person remarks in this chapter are Allen's) remembered having read it years ago, and when Robert and I decided to collect and document our study techniques, I suggested this book. It explains that, although most people have learned elementary reading, very few have learned what the authors call "inspectional reading" and "analytical reading." The schools simply don't teach it, although they should. This sort of reading is what you need in order to understand books like the Course, or books of philosophy—books that are presenting ideas rather than just facts or entertainment, or telling a story.

I discovered that many of the things that Adler and Van Doren's book recommends are exactly what I have been doing with the Course, and reading this book has helped me to identify what they are. I believe it can help anyone become a better reader. By that I don't mean it is a book about reading as a basic skill. *How To Read A Book* will help you process what you read and absorb it more rapidly. Its advice applies to any book. *Bringing the Course to Life* is a specific application of these same techniques to *A Course in Miracles*, and adds several techniques which are completely unique to the Course.

Familiarizing Yourself with the Text

In general, Adler and Van Doren recommend reading a book in two phases: superficially, and analytically. Such advice, we believe, is definitely applicable to reading the Course, and can greatly ease your introduction to the Text.

First, read *superficially*

First – and the authors say this is critical – you should read the material *superficially*. I did exactly that when I first read the Text, reading the entire book in one month. No way did I understand it all. There were lots of parts that meant absolutely nothing to me. I just brushed on by them. The idea in a first read-through like this is to read quickly, and to understand everything you *can* understand without extra effort. You are going for just what is easily within your grasp and nothing more.

It is vital in this kind of superficial reading *not* to stop and struggle with something you don't understand. If you do you'll never get through the book. Just breeze on by it. Even if you never do more than read the Text this once, superficially, and understand no more than thirty percent of it that way, isn't thirty percent of the whole book better than one hundred percent of nothing? If you never read the whole book, one hundred percent of nothing is all you will have.

There are 669 pages in the Text. Reading just ten pages a day will take you through the book in 67 days, or just over two months. If you read superficially, as I am suggesting here, you will only be spending two to three minutes per page, or even less if you are a rapid reader. The entire Text has been put on cassette tape, read aloud; it occupies approximately 37.5

hours of tape. That means that if you took just one hour a day and read the book *aloud*, you could read it in a little over one month. Surely, reading silently, you can read even faster than that! Remember, the goal of this superficial read-through is just picking up whatever you can.

The result of such a read-through is that you gain an overall feel for the whole Text. When you read the later parts, the earlier parts will still be fairly fresh in your mind. By reading it in a compressed amount of time, as opposed to stretching out a reading over years, you will find that you will make associations between different parts of the book that you would not have made before. Once you have done such a read-through, you will find that the slower, analytical reading of one section at a time becomes easier.

The idea of superficial reading also applies to the study of a chapter in the Text. As I lead a Text class, when we start a new chapter, I always read it through several times completely. At least twice. When I used to commute by car, I bought the Course on tape (fairly expensive but worth it if you have a regular time to listen). I would use the tapes of the Course and listen to each chapter several more times while I was commuting in my car. My purpose was to get a general feel for the entire chapter. Often, I found that I picked up on things while listening that I completely overlooked while reading. Only when I felt I had a grasp of the whole chapter would I step down to the section level and start digging into a single section.

There, once again, I would read the entire section several times before I began to make any notes on it. Usually, by the time I got down to the line-by-line level, I had a pretty good understanding of what the section was all about, and therefore the details had a framework upon which to fit.

For someone who is not a teacher, but a serious student, I would recommend doing a superficial reading of the Text every year or two, to keep familiar with the whole Text. And if you are taking part in a study group or Text class, I would recommend superficial reading of each chapter as you begin it and also as you end it (reading after the detailed study cements and ties together what you learned during that study), and also reading through each section two or three times before beginning the line by line study.

If this sounds like a lot of reading, I want to emphasize that all we are talking about here is *superficial* reading, as fast as you can. Reading a three-page section should not take more than ten minutes at most; you could read it aloud in that time. Many people will find they can read through three pages in six minutes or less. You won't believe how much your understanding increases through this simple practice.

Second, read *analytically*

The analytical reading, which is the subject of the rest of this book, is what happens in detailed study. The principal method of analytical reading is to ask the book questions and to find the answers to the questions. You have to both *ask* and *answer* the questions. This kind of reading is very involving. When you notice relationships between two paragraphs in the section, draw a line in the Text, or write references in the margin, to remind you of the relationship.

With this kind of reading we need to proceed as slowly as is necessary to gain a thorough understanding. Many study groups read through a section once, discuss it haphazardly, and move on, without ever really coming to grips with the content of the section. We are in a hurry to get finished. If we slow down, we feel discouraged to think that, if we take just one section a week to study, we will require about five years to complete it. That's one of the benefits of the read-through; it takes the edge off thoughts like, "I'll never finish it!" or "I can't wait to see what it says about relationships." If we have read the Text all the way through, we feel more relaxed about slowing down to really dig into each section. We don't feel that urgent need to press on quickly, wondering what is ahead, because we already *know* what is ahead.

Marking the Text

In studying anything, we often want to mark the material in some way. The Text, in particular, invites such marking. If you are like me, you may end up with two copies of the Course: one that you mark up, and a second that you do not mark. I use the unmarked copy for my read-throughs, so that I am free to see what I am reading in a new light, rather than having my marks pull me into seeing the same things I saw the last time I read the passage.

Besides the obvious desire to highlight a passage simply because we like it, or to help us find something we find particularly significant, there are other good reasons to want to mark the Text. For instance, when a particular word or phrase recurs over and over in a section or within a chapter, I like to go through and highlight or underline every occurrence of the word or phrase in a special color. Examples that come to mind are the word "guilt" in Chapter 13, or the term "Holy

Spirit" in Chapter 5. Marking them all with a special color makes it easy to scan through and examine each reference to the idea, which is especially useful in teaching.

Another reason for marking is writing down cross-references. When you begin to realize how often the Text refers to itself, and how often there are related topics you want to connect somehow (for instance, linking all the mentions of the idea, "There is no order of difficulty in miracles"), you will find yourself wanting to write references to related passages in the margin.

A third reason for marking is simply making notes. When you get an "Aha!" about the meaning of some paragraph or sentence, jot your thoughts in the margin. It will help you remember what you now understand when you read the passage again at a later time.

However, there is a problem with marking. In the one-volume combined edition, the paper is very thin, like Bible paper. Normal highlighters and ballpoint pens will bleed through the page and show on the other side, which can be confusing. I can offer a few suggestions that may help to make your marking experiences happier ones.

Colored pencils

Try using colored pencils, instead of highlighters, to highlight or otherwise mark the Text. There is even a yellow highlighter *pencil* that is available, which does a decent job of standing out; often, Christian or Bible bookstores will carry them, since students of the Bible have the same desire to mark and the same problem with thin paper. Ordinary colored pencils can work well also. The drawbacks to pencils are that they are hard, their points often sharp; you will probably make a groove in the page by marking because you must press on the pencil, and there is some risk of tearing the page. A second drawback is that the marking is fainter than the normal highlighter pens, and therefore less obvious when you are searching for something.

Highlighters recommended for FAX paper

There are a few highlighter pens that indicate (usually on the barrel or elsewhere on the package) that they are meant for use with fax paper, which is thin, and has the same bleed-through problem that Bible paper has. They cost the same as regular highlighters, and come in multiple colors, although I often have trouble finding anything but yellow. These markers do not bleed through. I have found these in large office supply stores, and also sometimes in Christian bookstores.

Drafting pens

Most art supply stores, and some stationery stores, will carry refillable drafting pens which use India ink. That kind of ink, which consists of fine particles suspended in water (rather than a stain), will not soak into the paper and bleed; the color stays on the surface. Thus, these pens are ideal for underlining and making notes on thin paper. They come with very fine metal tips, as well; the fine line they make is another advantage in the small margins. The drawback to these pens is that the ink dries quickly and dries hard. That's good for what you write, but if you do not use the pen for a few days, it tends to clog easily. Filling the pen and cleaning it can be messy. I like to use this kind of pen when I am making a lot of notes over a short period of time, but otherwise it is too much trouble.

A close second best are the ultra-fine felt- or plastic-tipped pens, the non-refillable, disposable kind. These are similar to Pilot or roller ball pens, but with much thinner tips and special inks. You will find these in art supply stores. They come in many colors, and there are several brands. Look for pens that indicate the measurement of their tip, such as .01 mm or even .005 mm. You may see something like "005" on the top of the cap. If in doubt, ask the store clerk, and tell them you want ultra-fine tips and ink that will not bleed.

Plastic ruler

An invaluable tool for marking the Text is a short, plastic ruler. I carry a flat magnifier ruler, available in many bookstores, that is intended for reading fine print. It fits between the pages and serves as a good bookmark, as well. My main use for it, though, is drawing lines! I use it when underlining the Text, to make the lines neat. I sometimes use it to draw a fine line between two phrases on a page when I want to call my attention to the way they are related or linked to one another. For instance, if one paragraph raises a question that is answered a few paragraphs later (on the same page or the next page), I often will draw a line connecting them when I discover the link. A piece of cardboard, or anything with a straight edge, will serve the same purpose. Don't draw lines with ballpoint pens however; they will smear. Use the drafting pens, or pencils.

You Will Understand It

As you begin to read the Text, be comforted in knowing that nearly everyone who reads it finds it hard to understand at first. Besides the resistance of the ego to understanding the

Holy Spirit's message, the language the Course uses is definitely more difficult to understand than your average daily newspaper. The ideas being presented are profound. The discussions of the devious strategies of the ego, which the Course insists we need to expose to the light before we can let them go, can be complex and confusing. They are *meant* to be confusing; the ego does not want you to understand its game.

The author of the Course recognizes the difficulty beginners have, and he addresses the issue in the following paragraph, from Chapter 22:

> Of all the messages you have received and failed to understand, this course alone is open to your understanding and can be understood. This is *your* language. You do not understand it yet only because your whole communication is like a baby's. The sounds a baby makes and what he hears are highly unreliable, meaning different things to him at different times. Neither the sounds he hears nor sights he sees are stable yet. But what he hears and does not understand will be his native tongue, through which he will communicate with those around him, and they with him. And the strange, shifting ones he sees about him will become to him his comforters, and he will recognize his home and see them there with him. (T-22.I.6)

Think of how things must appear to a baby who has not yet learned to talk. All around her are these "strange, shifting ones," who keep putting their faces in front of her and making odd sounds with their mouths. Sometimes she thinks the sounds mean something. Sometimes she thinks they mean something else. Sometimes she is sure the sounds are meaningless (and sometimes they are!). She is confused. When she tries to make her wishes known with her own sounds, she does not get the results she wants, and cries. Sometimes crying seems to work the best.

Yet somehow, through that confused and muddled process, the baby eventually learns to talk, and to understand those who are talking to her. The strange, incomprehensible sounds eventually become her native tongue. She speaks it and understands it without even thinking about it most of the time.

The comforting idea for us is that we are like babies in learning the Course. There is much we do not understand yet, but that is perfectly natural. Relax, let the process take its course, and eventually this strange language of the spirit will become your native tongue, as much a part of you as is the language you learned as a child.

You *will* understand!

Chapter 4

An Overview of the Techniques

Read slowly and think about

To begin with, let us give an overview of the techniques. One way to view them all is as expansions of a very simple thought, presented in the Introduction to Part II of the Workbook:

> They should be slowly read and thought about a little while. (W-pII.In.11:4)

The key points here are *read slowly* and *think about what you read*. All too often we are barreling along, trying to finish a certain number of pages in a certain time. That's fine when you are simply reading through the Text for a general feel of the contents – something we recommend doing periodically. To achieve an in-depth understanding that allows us to take its message deeply into our lives, however, we need to slow down and think about what we are reading. We need to ask ourselves: Do we understand it? If not, are there clues nearby to help us discern the meaning? Let related thoughts come. "If this statement is true, what else does that imply?"

Another similar thought is given in Review IV of the Workbook:

> Let each word shine with the meaning God has given it, as it was given to you through His Voice. Let each idea…give you the gift that He has laid in it for you to have of Him. (W-pI.rIV.7:4–5)

The words of the Course have come to us from God through His Voice, the Holy Spirit. Each thought has a gift to give us; our task is to let the meaning of the words shine for us, and impart their gift to us. That takes time and thought. It means reading slowly, and thinking about what we read.

In studying any passage in the Course, we recommend at least two readings. Read straight through once, without stopping, to familiarize yourself with the passage. Then, read a second time, slowly, thinking about what you read and using the study techniques to draw out more of the meaning.

In a sense, all of the techniques in this book can be seen as examples of one simple practice: As you read, ask yourself questions, and let the text you are reading answer your questions. I (Allen) have found it helpful to identify three categories of questions, or three steps (based on Bible study techniques I learned years ago). They are: Observation, Interpretation, and Application. The techniques we are offering will be grouped into these three steps as an aid to remembering them. In general, the techniques will be applied in the order of these three steps, although that should not be considered a strict rule; often, the insights gained in a later step will illuminate an earlier step.

I. Observation: What does it say?

The first step is observing what the text says. Here, you are simply noticing various things about what you are reading, such as the kind of sentence (statement, question, injunction); the central thought of the sentence (subject, verb and object); key terms; repeated phrases and words; connective words like "and" or "but"; and terms and concepts which have been mentioned in nearby paragraphs or sections. Observation is primarily gathering the raw material for the Interpretation and Application steps that follow, although sometimes Observation is enough to trigger a new understanding.

Observation techniques include:

A. *Notice the kind of sentence*

B. *Notice what is not said and questions that arise*

C. *Notice the subject, verb, and object of the sentence*

D. *Notice pronouns*

E. *Notice key terms*

F. *Notice repeated words and phrases*

G. *Notice when imagery and figures of speech are used*

H. *Notice connective words*

I. *Notice capitalized words*

J. *Notice italicized words*

K. *Notice terms, phrases and concepts from recent paragraphs*

II. Interpretation: What does it mean?

The second step goes beyond the simple observation of what is said to what is *meant* by what is said. You make sure you understand the meaning of key terms such as "Atonement," and that you know what all the pronouns refer to. You try rewording a sentence in your own words, or to summarize its meaning. You allow related thoughts to come. If logic is being used, you follow the logic, and see if it is persuasive to you. You notice the connections and let the meaning of those connections sink in. You may locate a key sentence, identify the central thought of a passage, or try summarizing an entire section. You are working with definitions of words, with the meaning of sentences, their interconnectedness, the reasons for their presence, and with the implications of what is said that go beyond what is explicitly stated.

In Interpretation, which is the core of study, you are trying to recreate the author's thought in your own mind. Words, as the Course itself tells us, are an imperfect communication medium. Complex, multi-faceted thoughts are reduced to mere symbols on paper. The purpose of Interpretation is to connect with the meaning behind the words so that the original thought that inspired them is born again in your mind.

Interpretive techniques include:

A. *Be context-sensitive; notice the connections*
B. *Plug in the meaning of terms, phrases, and pronouns*
C. *Get the meaning of the sentence*
    i. *Reduce the sentence to its basic gist or essence*
    ii. *Reword the sentence to express this gist*
    iii. *Let related ideas come to help the meaning sink in*
D. *Follow the logic*
E. *Recognize when a passage is addressing a specific situation, issue or belief*
F. *Identify irony and statements of false arguments*
G. *Understand and appreciate biblical references*
H. *Summarize the message*

III. Application: What does it mean to me?

Here, in the third step, you bring the words of the Course into direct contact with your life. You attempt to experience, or perhaps visualize, what the passage is talking about; many images in the Course lend themselves to this practice. You read it as personally addressing you, perhaps changing "you" statements into "I" statements. You attempt to carry out specific instructions that might be given. You dialogue with the author, asking him questions or turning what you read into a prayer. You relate the principles given to specific areas in your life: your needs, problems and concerns.

Application means literally bringing the Course to life – to *your* life. It is applying the thoughts you have read to situations you are currently experiencing. It means taking the message personally. It means taking general and abstract ideas and making them concrete. It means following the instructions given to you in the Course.

Application techniques include:

A. *Experience and visualize the passage*
B. *Read the passage as personally addressing you*
    i. Engage in a dialogue with the author
    ii. Put what you are reading into the first person form
    iii. Turn what you are reading into a prayer
    iv. Insert your name in appropriate places
    v. Respond to instructions that are given
    vi. Read it as if Jesus is talking to you
C. *Identify in yourself thoughts or states of mind the Course speaks about*
D. *Apply what you are reading to the specifics of your life*

Not all of these techniques will apply to any given sentence or paragraph; you will need to pick and choose among them as you read. But every sentence and paragraph will be brought to life through some of these techniques. Above all, always remember that you have the Holy Spirit as your Teacher. Ask His help in applying these techniques; ask Him to speak to you, personally, through the words of the Course.

The rest of this book will consist of looking at these study techniques, in the order given above. The observation techniques we will look at first are probably the least exciting, since they are mainly laying the groundwork for the interpretation and application that will follow, but we hope that even these basic tools will prove immediately helpful in your study.

In describing the techniques, we will be using abundant examples. It therefore may be helpful to have your Course book out so that you can open it to the various examples we use.

Chapter 5

Step 1. Observation
Techniques A-G

As we said in the previous chapter, the first element of study is Observation. The essence of this step is simple: We just look closely at the words we are reading.

This step is helpful when reading anything, but crucial when reading the Course. Many of us are accustomed to brushing our eyes over a page to get the gist of a paragraph. We give the specific words and phrases no more than a passing glance, for our goal is to take in the overall idea they express. It is as if we don't want to pay too close attention to the trees for fear of missing the forest.

The Course does not work this way. If you stand back at a distance and ignore the individual trees, ironically, you will also miss the forest. In the Course, *the overall idea emerges from a careful inspection of the details.* In reading the Course, then, one of the main injunctions is to *notice*. All of our observation steps begin with that important word: "notice." Be highly aware of the words you are reading. Don't just brush over the individual words on your way to grasping the gist. Instead of rushing past the form to get the content, look at the form. Notice it, in all its detail. Beware of your mind's temptation to select out certain words, phrases or sentences as irrelevant. Instead, notice everything. Be aware of every word, every punctuation mark.

In this chapter and the next we will cover the observation techniques. We will warn you ahead of time that these are probably the least interesting of the techniques. People generally find Interpretation and Application to be far more fascinating. But Observation remains the foundation on which they rest.

A. Notice the kind of sentence

Simply notice whether each sentence is a statement, a question, an exclamation, or an injunction (a direction to do something). This is usually quite simple to do, but sometimes it can get a little tricky.

Examples:

i. A statement

> Temptation has one lesson it would teach, in all its forms, wherever it occurs. (T-31.VIII.1:1)

A statement simply tells us something or makes an assertion. Its purpose is to communicate its thought to us.

ii. A question

> How do you make the choice? (T-31.VIII.2:1)

A question can be one of three kinds. The first kind, as

seen above, poses a question to be answered by the Course itself in the following sentences. When you see such a question, mentally note it, and look for the answer in the material that comes after it.

The second kind of question is a question *of the readers*, which we, the readers, are expected to answer in our own minds. For instance:

> How do you feel? Is peace in your awareness? Are you certain which way you go? And are you sure the goal of Heaven can be reached? (T-23.II.22:8-11)

This kind of question is meant to direct us inward, to reflect on what our answer really is. So, when you notice them, ask these questions of yourself very personally. Their purpose is to get you in touch with what you are thinking and feeling, and to engage you in dialogue. Sometimes they uncover painful and even ludicrous things that occupy the space of your mind. Let them serve that purpose.

A third kind of question, very common in the Course, is what is often called a *rhetorical* question, one to which no answer is required, often because the answer is so obvious. For example:

> Would you not rather that all this [sin] be nothing more than a mistake, entirely correctable, and so easily escaped from that its whole correction is like walking through a mist into the sun? (T-19.II.8:1)

> Can you believe a shadow can hold back the Will that holds the universe secure? (T-24.In.1:8)

Although no answer is expected, the rhetorical question is there for a reason. It points out to us something that is patently obvious, but which we may not have *realized* is so. The first question above, for instance, is intended to make us realize that we really *would* prefer that sin be no more than an easily correctable mistake. Thus, when we encounter such a question, our response might be simply to pause for reflection and consciously acknowledge the truth of what is said.

iii. An exclamation

> How beautiful it is to walk, clean and redeemed and happy, through a world in bitter need of the redemption that your innocence bestows upon it! (T-23.IN.6:5)

Exclamations are often a call to our emotions and feelings. They signify to us an appropriate emotional response to what is being discussed. When we see exclamations, we may want (as part of what we are calling Step III, Application) to attempt to evoke that feeling within ourselves.

iv. An injunction

> Be never fearful of temptation, then, but see it as it is; another chance to choose again. (T-31.VIII.4:2)

Injunctions tell us to do something, and the Course is filled with them. It is important to read them not as mere ideas, but as instructions to be carried out. The above passage, for instance, is not just saying that temptation is really another chance to choose again. It is giving us an instruction: "Never be afraid of temptation. Instead, *see* it as another chance to choose again." Imagine what would happen if we actually carried this instruction out and made it a habit in our daily life.

B. Notice what is not said and questions that arise

This means noticing, first of all, questions that arise in our own minds, and then looking for the answers, either in what follows or what has come before. For instance, the Text's final section mentions "the saviors of the world" (T-31.VIII.4:4), but does not tell us who these saviors are. Noticing this, and asking the question, may send us back to the previous section, "The Savior's Vision," for our answer.

Furthermore, notice your mind's reactions to what you are reading: What seems unclear? What statements arouse resistance in you? What parts seem muddled or empty of real meaning?

These are passages to which you will need to pay particular attention in order to grasp their meaning and purpose. We have found that when something seems unclear, out of place, or unrelated to the main topic under discussion, it is usually because we are missing something that truly *is* there on the page. With further study we find that the meaning becomes clear; the reason for a "digression" becomes apparent; and the sentence or paragraph we thought out of place is really related to the context – we had just overlooked the connection.

The Course is packed with meaning, and every bit of it has a purpose. Nothing is there by mistake:

> You are studying a unified thought system in which nothing is lacking that is needed, and nothing is included that is contradictory or irrelevant. (W-pI.42.7:2)

Unlike normal writing, in the Course, *nothing is included that is irrelevant.* The author of the Course seems to be speaking from a vast and unified structure of thought he is holding in his mind. As he speaks, if some of his statements seem out of context, it is not because his mind is wandering, but because we have missed the unifying structure.

Therefore, we suggest that when you encounter something that seems out of place or difficult to understand, make a note of it. You might write it down as a question to the author: "Why are you talking about forgiving the past in the middle of this discussion about the real world?" By making your questions and lack of understanding conscious, you are preparing your mind to receive the answer.

Example 1:

> Temptation has one lesson it would teach, in all its forms, wherever it occurs. (T-31.VIII.1:1)

The question may occur as you read this, what is the "one lesson" being referred to? By raising this question, your mind becomes poised to notice the answer, which is right in the next sentence.

Example 2:

In "The Special Function" (T-25.VI), the first paragraph speaks of how a forgiving person sees the world. In the second paragraph, the author begins talking about how eyes grown accustomed to dimness are pained by the light of brilliant day. We may wonder, "Why is he talking about this here? What does this have to do with forgiveness?" Notice those questions in your mind, write them down if you wish, and then read on. You may find the answer in what follows; you may need to come back and look more carefully at what you've already read. In this example, you will hopefully discover that the image of eyes shrinking from light is a metaphor for our resistance to *really* seeing, to seeing the world through forgiving eyes – which, of course, was the topic of the first paragraph.

The important part of this technique is simply making a note of your questions and lack of understanding as you become aware of them, and then being on the lookout for the answers.

C. Notice the subject, verb, and object of the sentence

This technique may bring back unpleasant memories of grade school and high school and even, for some of us older folks, memories of diagramming sentences. Paying attention to the basic structure of a sentence, however, can really help clarify complex sentences, of which there are a great many in the Course.

As you probably remember from school, the *subject* of a sentence is the doer, the one taking some action. The *verb* is the action the subject is taking, and the *object* is the thing being acted upon. For instance: "John threw the ball." "John" is the subject, "threw" is the verb, and "ball" is the object.

Example 1:

Let's look at T-31.VIII.1:1 again: "Temptation has one lesson it would teach, in all its forms, wherever it occurs." Although the word order is turned around a bit, you can see that the subject is "Temptation." The verb is "would teach" (in other words, "desires to teach" or "aims to teach"). (Strictly grammatically speaking, "has" is the main verb of this sentence, but "would teach" is the verb that really conveys the central point of the sentence) The object is "one lesson." "Temptation…would teach…one lesson." The rest of the sentence is additional, explanatory material (which is covered by later techniques). Boiling the sentence down to its bare bones of subject, verb, and object lays bare its central meaning: Temptation always tries to teach one particular lesson. Notice how this enhances Technique B, the one we just discussed. Having grasped that temptation's only purpose is to teach a particular lesson, your mind naturally asks, "What is that lesson?" Now you can be on the lookout for the answer, which comes in the next sentence: "It would persuade the holy Son of God he is a body" (T-31.VIII.1:2).

Example 2:

The following passage is an example of a more complex sentence with a very simple subject, verb and object:

> Trials are but lessons that you failed to learn presented once again, so where you made a faulty choice before you now can make a better one, and thus escape all pain that what you chose before has brought to you.
>
> (T-31.VIII.3:1)

The main subject, verb and object are, simply: "Trials are lessons." The remainder of the sentence explains what kind of lessons they are, the purpose of those lessons, and the outcome of learning them.

We will come back to this in Technique C of Interpretation, where we suggest that one way to distill the gist of a sentence is to attempt to state its essential meaning in your own words. Identifying the subject, object and verb is a great help in doing that. Just isolate the framework of the sentence as we've done above, and then put it in your own words.

Incidentally, if you are lucky enough to have been taught how to diagram sentences, and still remember how to do it, we recommend that you brush up on it. With sentences you are having a hard time understanding, go beyond merely identifying subject, verb, and object, and diagram the entire sentence. It can be a great aid to understanding.

D. Notice pronouns

The Course makes extensive, and often confusing, use of pronouns. Pronouns are like little puzzles that need to be solved in order to understand the complete meaning of what is being said. In this observation step, we are just noticing them; in the interpretation step we will try to determine the nouns they refer to.

Examples:

> It would persuade the holy Son of God he is a body, born in what must die, unable to escape its frailty, and bound by what it orders him to feel. (T-31.VIII.1:2)

There are several pronouns here: "it," "he," "its," "it" again, and "him." We need to determine what each pronoun refers to in order to properly understand the sentence. We'll return to this in Technique A of Interpretation.

The next example contains some pronouns whose referents are a bit more difficult to determine:

> Their Presence is obscured by any veil that stands between Their shining innocence, and your awareness that it is your own and equally belongs to every living thing along with you. (T-26.X.2:7)

Here we have "Their" twice, "your" twice, "it," and "you." To show how difficult it can be to identify the nouns for these pronouns, the meaning of "Their" can only be gleaned from the previous section, "For They Have Come." In that section, "They" refers to God and Christ.

If we do not really notice these pronouns, and ask ourselves what they mean, we can quite easily read through a sentence without really gaining any understanding of what it said.

E. Notice key terms

By key terms we mean terms that are given special meaning by the Course, either throughout its length or in just one or two sections. Noticing these terms (which is part of Observation) and understanding their special meaning (part of Interpretation) are essential. If your mind assigns them their more normal meaning, you may completely misunderstand what the Course is saying. For instance, if you think "God's Son" always refers to Jesus Christ, then the sentence, "In the calm light of truth, let us recognize that you believe you have crucified God's Son" (T-13.II.5:1), seems to be saying we believe we crucified Jesus. Since none of us actually believes that (unless we happen to believe we had a past life as a Roman centurion), the Course seems to be saying something absurd.

Our first task is just to notice these terms. This can be quite a job in itself. Often we may not realize that a common English word is being given special meaning until we see it repeat again and again within a few paragraphs. *A Course Glossary* (written by Robert) includes most such terms, and so using it can help us learn to notice them.

Examples:

The phrase, "holy Son of God" (T-31.VIII.1:2), is a key phrase in the Course. It refers, not to any one individual, such as Jesus, nor to some male divine figure, but to our shared Identity as God's creation, the Christ, sinless, perfect and innocent – a limitless spiritual being. The words "Son of God," "God's Son," and "Christ" all have pretty much the same meaning.

The sentence quoted above, therefore, is properly understood when we know this meaning of the term "God's Son." We believe we have crucified (or killed) the holy Self God placed in us at creation. We believe we are no longer what God created us to be, but the crippled and corrupted being we have made of ourselves.

There are many such examples of specialized use of terms and phrases in the Course. Nearly every term borrowed from Christian theology – *sin, atonement, salvation, Holy Spirit, Heaven,* and, most especially, *forgiveness* – is redefined by the Course. Likewise, many psychological terms – *ego, projection, denial,* and *dissociation* – are either redefined or used with specific meanings that are not familiar to the general reader.

If you are new to the Course you need to be aware that you are walking through a terrain in which everything you see *looks* familiar but much of it is actually new and unique. Be aware that with every significant word you see, the Course will at least give it a deepened meaning and quite possibly a significantly *different* meaning. The observation technique in this regard is to simply notice terms as you read, and realize that they may not mean what you think they do.

F. Notice repeated words and phrases

Read through the section being studied and notice words or phrases that are frequently repeated. You may even want to mark such key terms with different colored pencils or highlighters. This may, in fact, prove to be one of the most helpful study techniques you will find in relation to the Course.

The repetition of a word or phrase is giving you a clue as to the main focus of the section you are reading. The repetition of the words "revelation" and "miracles" in T-1.II, for instance, shows you that these two words represent major topics in this section. Reading over the section will make it clear they are being contrasted, and you may find it helpful to mark the occurrences of the terms, and then write down all the ways in which they are contrasted.

Another thing that observation of repeated words and phrases can tell you is what is important to understand. The term "choose," for instance, is a key term in T-31.VIII. Some variation of it ("choose," "choice," "chose") occurs in the title and in seventeen other places in the section. Noticing this frequency, you will be alerted to try to understand just exactly what kind of choice you are being asked to make.

Sometimes the repetition of a word or set of words may extend over many sections of the Text. This should be a clue to you that the sections are all closely related in some way. For instance, the words "faith, belief and vision" occur together often throughout the section by that title, T-21.III. A careful reader will notice, in addition, that they recur quite often in the following section as well, where the word "reason" is added into the mix. This ties the two sections together. The word "reason" then crops up repeatedly all the way through until the fifth section of Chapter 22.

Marking the words with some color code can help you to scan through the sections and to arrive at a fuller understanding of what the Course means by reason, for instance, and how it is related to faith, belief and vision. The *Concordance for A Course in Miracles* (compiled by The Foundation for Inner Peace) or the electronic version of the Course with searching software (produced by CenterLink), which is available for both PC and Macintosh computers, can be a great help in finding repeated words and phrases. Both are available from The Foundation for Inner Peace.

G. Notice when imagery and figures of speech are used

The Course makes rich use of images, symbols, and figures of speech. Before we can understand and appreciate these, we first must notice them. This is often easy. At times, however, the Course will subtly build an image over several sentences or paragraphs. In such passages, one may spot scattered, fragmentary images without realizing they are parts of a single whole.

Example:

> Let us be glad that we can walk the world, and find so many chances to perceive another situation where God's gift can once again be recognized as ours! And thus will all the vestiges of hell, the secret sins and hidden hates be gone. And all the loveliness which they concealed appear like lawns of Heaven to our sight, to lift us high above the thorny roads we travelled on before the Christ appeared. (T-31.VIII.9:1-3)

In this passage we can readily see several images: "walk the world," "lawns of Heaven," "thorny roads." We may not realize, however, that they are part of a single overall picture. This becomes apparent only when we recognize that they are all walking images. Walking, lawns, roads – all are elements of a foot journey. Once we realize that, we can assemble the various pieces into a single image. That, however, goes beyond our present step of Observation and into Interpretation.

Sometimes an image, once established, will be utilized over and over again through the Course material. The image of "The Forgotten Song" (established in T-21.I) shows up again as "Heaven's song" in T-26.V.2:5 and T-26.V.5:4, and as the "Song of Prayer" in the supplement by that title. The word "song" occurs 58 times in the Course, and usually refers to this eternal song of love exchanged between God and God's creations. Being familiar with these images can enrich the meaning of every reference to "song."

The same is true with many other repeating images in the Course. Another image that runs through the Course is that of you and your brother, standing before a veil (sin, guilt) that is hiding the face of Christ from you. It is introduced in expanded form in "The Obstacles to Peace" (T-19.IV.D), and it pops up over and over again. Sometimes the reference to the image provides a major clue as to the meaning of the section in which the reference occurs.

Thus the Course does not simply use an image once and then discard it. Having established the image as a particular symbol, it uses that symbol to bring multiple layers of meaning into a discussion with just a few words. We are aware of no other book that does this so consistently. Recognizing and understanding the imagery of the Course is a major goal for any serious student.

Chapter 6

Step 1. Observation
Techniques H-K

H. Notice connective words

Connective words are those that in some way link together words, phrases, clauses or sentences. There are a number of different types:

- Simple conjunctions: *and, or, nor, but, for, yet*
- Correlatives: *either...or, neither...nor, both...and, not only...but [also]*
- Subordinating conjunctions: *that, when, where, while, because, so that, although, since, as, after, if, until*
- Conjunctive adverbs: *however, therefore, nevertheless, also, thus, then*
- Relative pronouns: *who, which, that*
- Transitional expressions: *yet, still, on the contrary, on the other hand, actually*

As we read, we need to pay special attention to these kinds of connective words, because they carry a great deal of meaning. Often, the richest meaning is to be found in the relationships they convey between sentences and between phrases within sentences. Sometimes, if we miss the connective words, we will completely misunderstand the meaning.

If this kind of very detailed study seems mechanical, or if it appears at first as if we are picking apart the Course, think again. We are not picking it apart; actually we are simply paying attention to the ways it is *linked together*, especially when we notice the connective words. We are reading slowly and thinking about what is said, and in doing so, we are uncovering meanings we might miss without this kind of careful study.

Example 1:

First, let's take a couple of simple connectives between three sentences, with fairly obvious meanings:

> Obey the Holy Spirit, and you will be giving up the ego.
> But you will be sacrificing nothing. On the contrary,
> you will be gaining everything. (T-7.X.3:8–10)

The first sentence makes the statement that if we obey the Holy Spirit, we will be giving up the ego. The second sentence begins with "but." Even though beginning sentences with "but" or "and" is not considered good writing, the Course does this constantly, and quite intentionally. In this case, separating the ideas into two sentences places a more distinct emphasis on the ideas in each one, and makes the contrast between them stronger.

Returning to the meaning of "but": It denotes contrast. In this case it carries the meaning of "contrary to expectation." Though you will be giving up the ego, *contrary to expectation* "you will be sacrificing nothing." This contrast carries a wealth of meaning. It implies that when the Holy Spirit asks us to give up the ego, we *expect* it to be a sacrifice. Yet it does not turn out that way. We find that we have sacrificed nothing because the ego *is* nothing.

Then comes the third sentence, starting with the transitional expression, "on the contrary." The meaning of that is pretty clear. But on the contrary to *what?* The key lies in our belief, expressed in the previous sentence, that giving up the ego means sacrificing something. On the contrary, answers the third sentence, "you will be gaining everything."

Example 2:

Next, let's look at an example of more subtle connective words between phrases in a single sentence:

> Trials are but lessons that you failed to learn presented once again, so where you made a faulty choice before you now can make a better one, and thus escape all pain that what you chose before has brought to you.
>
> (T-31.VIII.3:1)

We noted earlier in this series that the main thought of this sentence is, "Trials are lessons." The first clause in the sentence is telling us that when trials occur, they are really lessons we failed to learn in the past which are being "presented" to us once again.

The second clause begins with the word "so," a connective word. What does "so" mean? It seems to be understood here as: "so that." Thus, "so" means, "in order that," or, "for this purpose." It implies a relationship of *purpose* between the two clauses. There is a purpose behind the missed lessons of the past repeating for us. They are being presented to us again *in order that* "where you made a faulty choice before you now can make a better one."

The third clause of the sentence is introduced with another connective word: "thus." "Thus" means, "in this manner," or, "through this means." This word implies a relationship of *consequence or result* between the two clauses. By making the better choice mentioned in the second clause, you can, *as a result*, "escape all pain that what you chose before has brought to you." In other words, by repeating the lesson and making the correct choice this time, we can erase all the pain that arose from our past mistakes!

Notice the richness of meaning contained in those two little words, "so" and "thus." Trials are not merely missed lessons from the past randomly popping up again in our experience; they are being presented to us for a purpose – the idea of purpose is contained in that two-letter word, "so." Furthermore, as is shown in the connective word, "thus," by learning to make a better choice where before we made a faulty choice, we not only avoid additional pain; *we also escape from the pain caused by our past mistakes.* (**Note**: The word, "but," in the first part of the sentence, "Trials are but lessons," is not used as a connective word, in the common sense of "although" or "however." The Course often uses "but" with the meaning of "only" or "just," as in the phrase, "nothing but." Thus: "Trials are nothing but lessons....")

I. Notice capitalized words

In the Course, capitalized words other than the first word in a sentence indicate some reference to the divine. In the original editing of the Course, Helen Schucman was given general instructions about when to capitalize nouns and pronouns, but with some specifics. For instance, although she had a habit of capitalizing pronouns that refer to Jesus, she was told not to do so in the Course in order to emphasize his equality with us. Often, a capital letter on a noun or pronoun can be a key in understanding what the word refers to.

Example 1:

> It [temptation] would persuade the holy Son of God he is a body, born in what must die, unable to escape its frailty, and bound by what it orders him to feel.
>
> (T-31.VIII.1:2)

"Son of God" here refers to the one Son of Whom we are all a part, and not a particular individual such as Jesus. The phrase, "Son of God," is always capitalized, and even the phrase, "Sons of God," never occurs with a lowercase "s," thus emphasizing the essential divinity and unity of the Sons, even while clearly speaking of their apparent plurality. Since the Course tells us that "you are the Son of God" (W-pI.99.12:5), we can often take this as a reference to ourselves, we who, although we are together one Son of God, *think* we are distinct individuals with bodies.

In T-31.VIII.11:3, by paying attention to capitalization, we can tell that Jesus is addressing God the Father when he prays, "And can You fail in what is but Your Will?" If the words were not capitalized, it would seem that he was addressing us.

Example 2:

There are times when ordinary nouns are capitalized to indicate they are referring to the divine in some way. For instance:

> And they will meet with your invited Guests the miracle has asked to come to you. (T-28.III.8:8)

A little searching around will reveal that "Guests" here must refer to "your Father and your Self" two sentences earlier.

J. Notice italicized words

When the Course was being taken down by Helen Schucman, as she listened to the Voice speaking within her mind, it seemed to emphasize certain words. In her notes, she underlined those words to indicate the emphasis. Later, in the editing process, it was felt that too many words were emphasized, and so some of the underlining, which was translated into italic type when the Course was published, was removed. (This is related on page 366 of a book we recommend for every Course student: *Absence from Felicity*, by Kenneth Wapnick. It tells the story of Helen Schucman's scribing of the Course, and contains a great deal of material from Jesus that is not included in the Course.) The remaining italic words in the Course, of which there are many, still are meant to convey the emphasis given to those words by the Voice as Helen heard it, and often noticing that emphasis helps clarify or reinforce the meaning.

Example 1:

> *And do I want to see what I have denied **because** it is the truth?* (T-21.VII.5:14)

This entire sentence is italicized, and so the emphasized word in it is bolded, something that happens occasionally in the Course. Here, the emphasis on "because" is crucial to the impact of the sentence. It confronts us with a question: Do we want to see something we previously found threatening enough to deny, not because it feels good or pleases our ego, but simply because it is the truth. Without the emphasis on "because," the sentence might easily have no impact. With that emphasis, the sentence becomes quite confrontive.

Example 2:

In the following five sentences, the two italicized words help clarify a distinction the Course is trying to make. This distinction is between "you," that is, who you really are, and your "specialness," which is another way of describing the ego self you think you are, distinct from other ego selves. The fact that these two words are emphasized draws your attention to them. It makes it very clear that the Course is contrasting and clearly distinguishing "you" and the "specialness" you think you are:

> It is not *you* who are so vulnerable and open to attack that just a word, a little whisper that you do not like, a circumstance that suits you not, or an event that you did not anticipate upsets your world, and hurls it into chaos. Truth is not frail. Illusions leave it perfectly unmoved and undisturbed. But specialness is not the truth in you. *It* can be thrown off balance by anything.
> (T-24.III.3:1–5)

Example 3:

Sometimes, not too often, an entire sentence is italicized for emphasis. In such cases, we should realize that this sentence is meant to be seen as very important:

> Now the ego counsels thus; substitute for this another relationship to which your former goal was quite appro-

priate. You can escape from your distress only by getting rid of your brother....*Hear not this now!* (T-17.V.7:1,2,5)

There are innumerable instances of italicized words in the Course, probably five or six, at least, on every page. This is something a good student will pay close attention to in all his or her reading. One helpful practice when you see a sentence with an italicized word is to read that sentence aloud, giving special stress or emphasis to the italics. Hearing the stress on the word or words will help you get a clearer feel for the meaning they express.

One last note on italics: When an indented sentence (or series of sentences) or a paragraph is placed in italics, this is not for emphasis. It indicates that you are meant to repeat those lines to yourself. The "I" in such sentences is not the author of the Course, but you, the reader. In these cases, italics serve a useful purpose, but a different one from their usual purpose of indicating emphasis.

K. Notice terms, phrases and concepts from recent paragraphs

This requires reading a bit more widely than just the section you are currently studying. It is easiest when you are studying straight through a chapter, section by section. Here, you want to notice terms, phrases and concepts in the current section which are carrying on themes mentioned in earlier sections. Often, such terms and concepts have been defined or explained in detail in earlier sections, and are simply mentioned in later sections with the assumption that their meaning and significance are already clear to you. By being aware of what has been previously said, you can "plug in" the larger meaning from the earlier sections into what you are currently reading.

To carry out this step, simply look for how the sentence in front of you connects with what you have recently read. As you read, ask yourself, "How does this relate to what I have read recently? Does this sound like anything I have just read?" Take the words and ideas your eyes are on now, and cast a mental net behind you at the paragraphs and sections you have just read, and then see what gets caught in the net. After studying a paragraph for a while, you may wish to actually flip back a page or two and let your eyes skim over the material, looking for related words and thoughts. Look for the following things:

- *A common word or term.* Many of the key terms in any given sentence will have been weaving in and out of the preceding paragraphs. This is the best, easiest, and most frequent way to notice connections.
- *The same phrase or sentence.* The Course will occasionally use a phrase again or will even quote a whole sentence (such as "anger is never justified") from its previous material.
- *An image,* such as "clouds of guilt," "dark doors," "little spark," "treasure house," "golden circle," "face of Christ," etc.
- *An idea.* The author will frequently reference a previous idea without using the same language. This is a bit harder to spot.
- *Overtly identified reference.* Occasionally, the author comes right out and says, "we have said this before," "I have discussed this previously," etc.

Example 1:

When reading the final section of Chapter 31, "Choose

Once Again," we encounter the word "temptation" several times. This word has been frequently mentioned in earlier parts of Chapter 31 and even in the final section of Chapter 30, and has been defined in several ways. If you would like to come up with your own definition of the word, read over the following references: T-30.VIII.3:1–4; T-31.I.11:1; T-31.VII.10:1; T-31.VII.12:1. Our concise summary of those defining ideas is: *Temptation is not an involuntary pull toward pleasure, but a wish to make illusions real, particularly the wish to be a self you are not.*

Also, the Text has given us instructions on how to respond to temptation. See the following references: T-30.VIII.6:2–6; T-31.I.11:1–2; T-31.III.1:2–6; T-31.VII.14:1, 6. An overall summary of these instructions might be: *Respond to temptation by realizing it is your own wish to be a separate self, and that you truly do not want this, and need not feel guilty about it. Ask for a miracle to take its place.*

When, therefore, the word "temptation" is mentioned again in T-31.VIII.1:1, 4:2, 6:2 and 11:1, all that past discussion can be assumed to be part of what you know and understand about temptation. At times it will be helpful to plug in the definition that you have derived in place of the word itself, for instance:

> The wish to make illusions real and to be a self you are not has one lesson it would teach...It would persuade the holy Son of God he is a body. (T-31.VIII.1:1-2)

When you realize what the Course means by temptation, the words of this paragraph make a lot more sense. If you think temptation means just something like being enticed to steal something, for instance, you might have difficulty in seeing how this teaches that you are a body (of course it *does* teach that, but it isn't all that obvious). If, however, you realize that temptation is basically a wish to be a separate self, an ego, then its persuading you that you are a body makes perfect sense.

Example 2:

Right in this final section of the Text, 31.VIII, there are a few other examples of terms and phrases that have occurred significantly in earlier sections. The terms "image" and "images you make" (T-31.VIII.3:3; 4:1) refer to an extensive discussion of the images (or concepts) of the self that we have made. This was discussed a few sections earlier in T-31.V.1–3, and indeed all of Section V. The terms "savior" and "salvation" refer to the preceding section, "The Savior's Vision," T-31.VII. The term "lesson" was brought up in T-31.I. The discussion of "choosing" and our "choice" also started in that section (see 31.I.11:1–2), and is carried on through the whole chapter. Even the word "alternatives" in T-31.VIII.5:7 carries meanings begun in Section IV, "The Real Alternative," and carried on in T-31.VII.6:6 and T-31.VII.14:6.

Observing these interrelationships and recurring terms and phrases can be a great help in pulling together the complete picture of what the Course is teaching us. It isn't easy, at first. The more frequently you read over a chapter, the more connections and recurring ideas you will notice. This is why we often recommend, before beginning detailed study, that, as rapidly as you can, you read through, not only the section being studied, but those surrounding it, several times. If possible – if you are a rapid reader, especially – read the entire chapter several times. We also recommend setting yourself a regular program of reading through the Text, not just once, but over and over. It can be read entirely in one year just by reading two pages a day. Frequent and repeated reading is the best way to begin making yourself aware of these repeated themes and cross-references, which abound in the Course.

You may not yet have read the Text enough for repetitions of words and themes to just leap out at you. When you are studying a section of the Text, therefore, first read through the section being studied, and then take time to skim over the surrounding sections. Look for words and phrases from your main section that also show up in the surrounding sections, and see what light these other references may throw on your study section.

You may well feel that you will simply be unable to notice all the connections that are there. That is certainly true; they just keep going and going. However, the point is not to notice *all* of the connections. The point is simply to enrich your reading experience by noticing *more* connections than you do now. And everyone can do this.

Observation exercise

Let us now try to apply what we have learned about Observation. For this, we will use a paragraph that we will be using for many of the exercises in this book. It is Paragraph 3 of "Choose Once Again" (T-31.VIII), the last section of the Text:

> 1. Trials are but lessons that you failed to learn presented once again, so where you made a faulty choice before you now can make a better one, and thus escape all pain that what you chose before has brought to you. 2. In every difficulty, all distress, and each perplexity Christ calls to you and gently says, "My brother, choose

again." 3. He would not leave one source of pain unhealed, nor any image left to veil the truth. 4. He would remove all misery from you whom God created altar unto joy. 5. He would not leave you comfortless, alone in dreams of hell, but would release your mind from everything that hides His face from you. 6. His holiness is yours because He is the only Power that is real in you. 7. His strength is yours because He is the Self That God created as His only Son.   (T-31.VIII.3)

Read through the paragraph and then answer the following questions (we recommend writing your answers out on a separate sheet of paper):

1. Are there any sentences in this paragraph that are not statements (any questions, exclamations, or injunctions)?

2. Read through the paragraph and make note of what questions arise in your mind. You may want to jot these down here and see if they become answered in future exercises.

3. What is the subject, verb, and object of Sentence 4?

4. What is the most frequent pronoun used in Sentences 3-7?

5. Make a list of what you think are key terms in this paragraph.

6. Are there any repeating phrases in this paragraph?

7. What imagery is used?

8. What two connective words recur in Sentences 6 and 7?

9. Is "he" in Sentences 3-5 capitalized because of its meaning, or because it begins the sentence?

10. Are there any italicized words?

For the final question, open your book to the last section of the Text, "Choose Once Again." Read the first two paragraphs of that section and then read the third one again.

11. What key terms, phrases, and concepts from the first two paragraphs of this section occur again in the third paragraph?

ANSWER KEY

1. No, although the final part of Sentence 2, where Christ says, "My brother, choose again," is an injunction. Sentence 2 as a whole, however, is a statement.

3. The subject is "He." The verb is "would remove." The object is "misery."

4. He.

5. Here is our list: Trials, lessons, learn, choice/choose, pain, Christ, brother, image, veil, truth, misery, altar, dreams, hell, mind, His face, holiness, Power, strength, Self, God, created, His only Son.

6. "choice before/chose before," "God created," "He would not leave...He would," "His_____ is yours because He is the."

7. Images that veil the truth, altar unto joy, alone in dreams of hell, His face.

8. "Because" and "that."

9. Because of its meaning.

10. No.

11. *Terms*: lesson, Son, power, strength, Christ, hell, choose/choice.

Phrases: "choose again," "once again," "His strength."

Concepts: Temptation or trial as a lesson, Christ coming to you and asking you to choose again, remaining (or not remaining) in hell, the strength of Christ in you, which power (the body's or Christ's) is your real strength.

Chapter 7

Step II. Interpretation
A. Being Context-Sensitive

As we move into this second main category of study techniques, we need to briefly review what we mean by "interpretation." As we have pointed out before, observation and interpretation are very often done at the same time. We separate them into distinct steps only in order to clarify just what it is we do while studying. Therefore, just as you saw some interpretation mixed in with our descriptions and examples of observation, so too you will see some observation mixed in with the examples of interpretation.

This second step goes beyond the simple observation of what is said to the examination of what is *meant* by what is said. In Interpretation, which is the core of study, you are trying to recreate the author's thought in your own mind. Words, as the Course itself tells us, are an imperfect communication medium. Complex, multi-faceted thoughts are reduced to mere symbols on paper. The purpose of Interpretation is to combine your own mind with the words you are reading so that the original thought that inspired them is born again in your mind.

Interpretive techniques include:

A. *Be context-sensitive; notice the connections*
B. *Plug in the meaning of terms, phrases, and pronouns*
C. *Get the meaning of the sentence*
    i. *Reduce the sentence to its basic gist or essence*
    ii. *Reword the sentence to express this gist*
    iii. *Let related ideas come to help the meaning sink in*
D. *Follow the logic*
E. *Recognize when a passage is addressing a specific situation, issue or belief*
F. *Identify irony and statements of false arguments*
G. *Summarize the message*

We will now examine the first of these techniques in some detail.

A. Be context-sensitive; notice the connections

Perhaps the most important rule of Course Interpretation is this: *Be context-sensitive.* The reason that context is so essential is because of the Course's symphonic style, whereby themes are repeated and interwoven with other themes. This style makes for a dense web of interconnectedness. This web not only clarifies and enriches any given passage, it also provides a great deal of the Course's meaning. In other words, much of the Course's meaning is supplied by context, not direct statement.

Thus, to understand the full and accurate meaning of a

word, sentence or paragraph, one must have a sense for how it fits into its surrounding web. By itself its meaning will often be vague or flat. But in the context of the symphonic tapestry woven around it, its meaning becomes rich, subtle, profound, and crystal clear. Seeing how it fits into that web, then, is essential to the interpretive act. Thus, the reading habit of constantly *trying* to see how it fits is one of the primary habits a Course student must develop over time.

In other words, you will probably need to form a new reading habit. Forming this habit is fully within your power. If ordinary reading material was written like the Course, full of subtle references to preceding material, you would have already formed this reading habit long ago, and reading the Course would be easy. We can see this habit as consisting of two parts, observation and interpretation:

1. Look for the connections; notice terms, phrases and concepts from recent discussions.

This was the final step (K) of the Observation techniques. This step consisted of looking at the sentence in front of you and casting a mental net behind you, trying to see if any of this sentence's terms, phrases, images or concepts have cropped up in recent discussions.

Once you have uncovered a connection between your passage and another, you will want to ask yourself, "What exactly is the relationship between these two passages?" They might be referring to the exact same idea. Or they might be two variations on a common underlying theme (in which case, try to discover what that theme is). The relationship might be one of contrast; for instance, contrasting the ego's way with the Holy Spirit's. Or it might be one of cause and effect; one idea might logically follow from another. The attempt to uncover this relationship leads us into the next step.

2. See what light the context sheds on the passage you are reading.

Seeing how a passage connects with its surrounding material tells you exactly what its context is. Once you see this, you simply try to see the passage *in light* of its context. You ask yourself not just, "What does this mean?" but, "What does it mean *in this context?*" The guiding rule is to make sure that your interpretation of the passage harmonizes with its context; that your interpretation honors the web of connections you are seeing.

Example:

> In gentle laughter does the Holy Spirit perceive the cause, and looks not to effects. (T-27.VIII.9:1)

By itself, this sentence could mean all kinds of things. "The cause" could be almost anything, as could the "effects." Not knowing what these are, we have no clue why on earth the Holy Spirit is laughing.

Let us, then, look to this sentence's context. In this section ("The 'Hero' of the Dream" in Chapter 27), the "effects" (mentioned seven times in this section up to this point) are the physical world and all the things it does to us, all the ways it seems to attack us. Their "cause" (mentioned eleven times before in this section) is the *idea* of separation, an idea in the mind. In other words, the world's circumstances and events, which seem to cause us so much pain, are really just an effect of an idea in our mind. This idea, we are told, is literally a joke (this section, more than any other in the Course, is peppered with words like "laughter," "joke," and "jest"). If we only could see that our outer events and circumstances are merely pictures (or effects) of an underlying joke (the absurd idea of separation from God), they could have no effect on us.

Yet we do not see the world's underlying cause. We therefore see the world as its own cause, as self-existing and independently real. This makes its events seem extremely "serious," "heavy," and "sad" ("serious" has been mentioned three times in this section).

This is where the Holy Spirit comes in. His job is to correct our error of gazing in grief upon those "heavy" outer effects. In refreshing contrast, He looks only at their trivial cause and, seeing its absurdity, gently laughs. If only we can unite with His perspective, we will be free of all the heaviness we experience as we contemplate the events of our lives. Seeing with Him, we too can overlook the "serious" situations around us, as we look with Him at their ridiculous cause, and laugh.

If you now go back and read the sentence in question, it will probably mean a great deal more to you. In light of its context, it becomes a rather profound sentence, containing a liberating picture of both the Holy Spirit and of our condition in this world.

Being context-sensitive is *the* way to clear up confusing passages

Confusion is one of the most common experiences in reading *A Course in Miracles*. Even if you have read the Course for years you will frequently come upon passages that seem unclear. We do all the time. We have come to believe, however, that the exact meaning of almost every sentence in the Course can be uncovered simply by being highly sensitive to context.

What we mean by this, however, is virtually the reverse of how many Course students are sensitive to context. When a student comes across a confusing sentence, perhaps the most common method we see occurring is reading that sentence in the context of *one's overall understanding of the Course*. The student, in essence, asks herself, "Given my general understanding of the Course, what must this sentence mean?"

This way of being context-sensitive, we believe, largely results in projecting our own understanding onto any unclear passage. All we obtain from this is a miniature version of what we already thought. What we *don't* obtain is a fresh insight into what the author thought.

We believe we should go about it in the precise opposite way. We should read the sentence in light of its most *immediate* context and then gradually go out from there to more distant contexts, and finally to the larger context of the Course in its entirety. We see this in four steps:

1. Look closely at the immediate paragraphs surrounding the passage.

Usually, all the clues you need are right around the sentence in question, if you know how to look. The densely interwoven style of the Course may seem confusing, but one of its ultimate effects is incredible clarity. This style will scatter throughout the surrounding paragraphs dozens of references to the ideas of any given sentence. Through these references, you can view the same ideas from a cluster of slightly different angles. The net effect of this is exceptional clarity.

Therefore, look for these references. Look for recurrences of the terms, phrases, images and ideas in your sentence. Look for anything that relates to any part of your sentence. All of the things you find will be clues to its meaning. If you decipher these clues well, your interpretation will harmonize with all of these places. It will honor the entire web. If you come up with an incorrect interpretation, however, it will clash with most or all of the clues you have found. It will rip the web apart and leave dangling pieces lying all over. In short, your interpretation will be refuted from several angles at once.

This, we believe, is why the author can make the following claim: "I have made every effort to use words that are almost impossible to distort, but it is always possible to twist symbols around if you wish" (T-3.I.3:11). In light of how confusing the Course can be, this sentence can seem ludicrous. However, my experience is that when you learn how to be context-sensitive, distorting what the author is saying really does become "almost impossible."

Example:

Let's use a sentence that many Course students have puzzled over. Early in the Text, when the Course's use of terms is not yet completely consistent, it says, "the ego can learn." This is very uncharacteristic language for the Course. In fact, the Course says the opposite later on: "Therefore it [the ego] does not really learn at all. The Holy Spirit teaches you to use what the ego has made, to teach the opposite of what the ego has 'learned'" (T-7.IV.3:2-3). Though its language is unusual, what this phrase actually means is not difficult to ascertain if we look carefully at the clues right around it:

> p2. Many stand guard over their ideas because they want to protect **their thought systems** as they are, and **learning** means **change**. 2. **Change** is always **fearful** to the separated...because the separation was their first

experience of change. 4. You believe that if you allow no **change** to enter into your **ego** you will find peace.... 13. Nevertheless, **the ego can learn,** even though its maker can be misguided. 14. He cannot, however, make the totally lifeless out of the life-given.

p3. Spirit need not be **taught,** but the **ego** must be. 2. **Learning** is ultimately perceived as **frightening** because it leads to the relinquishment, not the destruction, of the **ego** to the light of spirit. 3. This is the **change** the **ego** must **fear**....

p4. 2. Refusing to **change** your mind will not prove that the separation has not occurred.... 7. If you are willing to renounce the role of guardian of **your thought system** and open it to me, I will correct it very gently and lead you back to God. (T-4.I.2-4)

We have put in boldface what we see as the relevant words – both the words in our phrase and words that are clearly linked to them. We put the phrase we are examining in bold, along with the words "ego" and "learn," since they are in that phrase. We put "change" in bold because it is linked with learning in the first sentence: "learning means change." We put words relating to "fear" in bold because fear is associated with learning and change. We put "your (or their) thought systems" in bold because it is connected with learning, change and fear, and because it functions as a rough synonym for "ego" here (as it does throughout the Text).

Looking at all of these clues, it is not terribly hard to interpret the phrase "the ego can learn." First, the words we have put in boldface are linked in very clear relationships: You guard *your thought system*, trying to keep out *learning*, because learning means *change* and change is something you *fear*. Second – and this is the crucial point – the same things that are said or implied about your *thought system* are also said about your *ego*. Just as you try to keep change from entering your thought system, so you try to "allow no change to enter into your ego" (2:4). Just as you *can* allow learning into your thought system (this is clearly implied), so "the ego can learn." Thus, "the ego can learn" means simply, "Learning and change can be allowed into your ego's thought system."

2. Then look at those passages in the surrounding pages that your sentence connects with.

Any unclarity that remains after the first step can often be dispelled by this second step. Search carefully the surrounding pages in the same way you searched the surrounding paragraphs. Look for other passages that use the same words, phrases, images and ideas as the one under examination. Very often this will yield one or a few specific passages that directly clarify the passage that is confusing you.

3. Then look at other discussions in the Course on the same topic.

If you are still unclear, try to find other discussions in the Course on this same topic. The consistency of the Course's thought on specific topics over hundreds of pages is truly remarkable. If your passage is about death, for instance, try to locate other discussions about death. This will usually be difficult to do without aids, but aids do exist. We would recommend especially the *Concordance of A Course in Miracles* and, for those with computers, the computer search programs put out for PC's and Mac's by CenterLink.

4. Throughout the process, use your overall understanding of the Course, but hold it lightly and loosely, letting it take a back seat to the three above contexts.

You will obviously be referencing your general Course understanding at every step. This is especially important for supplying the meaning of particular Course terms. However, we highly recommend that you let the more immediate contexts we have listed above be your primary guiding lights. They will show you, through dozens of clues, exactly what the author had in mind when he wrote that apparently puzzling passage. Through their guidance you will be able to directly contact his thought.

Using your overall understanding of the Course comes last in priority, we believe, because it leaves the most room for human error. One's overall understanding of the Course will always be somewhat in error. Further, deciding how to apply this broad understanding to a specific passage leaves room for further error. This approach also blocks you from receiving any new and fresh gifts this passage could give you. The passage itself becomes something of a blur, for you are not so much seeing *it*, as your preconceptions of what it *ought* to mean. You are covering it with your own mental paint, sealing in anything that might leap off the page and shake up your picture of things. The Course thus becomes little more than a projection screen. When overall understanding is kept in its proper place, instead of allowing your thinking to distort the Course, the Course will be able to correct your thinking.

Exercise in being context-sensitive

For this exercise, we will use the same paragraph as in the exercise from the previous chapter. As with all of the exercises in this book, this one is rather in-depth. We are not suggesting that you do this kind of detailed work with every paragraph in the Course. It is simply not practical. The purpose of these exercises is just to help develop your study skills and to show you the wealth of meaning that is waiting to be uncovered by those skills.

> 1. Trials are but lessons that you failed to learn presented once again, so where you made a faulty choice before you now can make a better one, and thus escape all pain that what you chose before has brought to you. 2. In every difficulty, all distress, and each perplexity Christ calls to you and gently says, "My brother, choose again." 3. He would not leave one source of pain unhealed, nor any image left to veil the truth. 4. He would remove all misery from you whom God created altar unto joy. 5. He would not leave you comfortless, alone in dreams of hell, but would release your mind from everything that hides His face from you. 6. His holiness is yours because He is the only Power that is real in you. 7. His strength is yours because He is the Self That God created as His only Son. (T-31.VIII.3)

In Question 11 from the previous exercise, we asked you to read this paragraph and the two immediately preceding it, looking for common terms, phrases and concepts. Here is the list we came up with:

Terms: lesson, Son, power, strength, Christ, hell, choose/choice.
Phrases: "choose again," "once again," "His strength."
Concepts: Temptation or trial as a lesson, Christ coming to you

and asking you to choose again, remaining (or not remaining) in hell, the strength of Christ in you, which power (the body's or Christ's) is your real strength.

Now let's try to discover the meaning that these connections add to our paragraph.

1. Temptation is always trying to teach you a lesson (1:1). Trials are presented to teach you a lesson (3:1). Trials and temptations are clearly similar (a trial might be defined as a situation in which you experience temptation), but are the two lessons similar? Is the first lesson (1:1) the same as the second lesson (3:1)? If not, what is their relationship?

2. Notice the words "power" and "strength" in 1:3 and 3:6-7. First, read 1:2-3, paying special attention to the words "power" and "strength." Then, read 3:6-7, again paying attention to the same two words. How did reading the first passage affect the meaning of the second? Did the first passage throw any light on the second? Try writing down the meaning you saw from putting both passages together.

3. 1:5 talks about choosing to remain in hell. 3:5 talks about how Christ would not leave you in hell. First, read both sentences, then see if the first throws any light on the second. Write down the picture that was produced by putting both together.

4. Notice the references to variations on the word "choose." Each time the word appears, there are two things that you are choosing between. What two things are you choosing between in 1:5? In 2:1-4? In 3:1? Take these three pairs of things and write down a version of "My brother, choose again," that includes them all and weaves them all together.

5. Notice how Christ comes to you twice in these three paragraphs, first in 1:4-5, then in 3:2. Are these two different kinds of appearances or two ways of describing the *same* appearance? If they describe the same appearance, try to write a version that combines both descriptions so as to better appreciate that appearance.

ANSWER KEY

1. The lesson temptation is trying to teach us is a lesson of the ego, the lesson that we are a body (1:2). The lesson that our trials are there to teach us is a lesson of Christ (3:2), a lesson that identifies us with Him (3:6-7). So the lessons are clearly different; opposite, in fact. We might even equate the lesson we are *tempted* to learn (1:1) with the unnamed thing in 3:1 that we taught ourselves before, when we failed to learn the true lesson, when we made a faulty choice that caused us pain.

2. I go through my life thinking that my body's tiny, frail power is the only strength I have. Yet my real strength is the unlimited power of Christ, Who is both my Self and God's only Son. My real strength is infinitely greater than what I think it is.

3. I have chosen to leave myself alone in hell, but Christ would not leave me there. He would come to me and save me from what I chose for myself. He would show me that the hell I am in is nothing but a self-made *dream* of hell. He would treat me far better than I have treated myself.

4. The three pairs of what you choose between are:

1:5	remaining in hell and holding everyone else there	taking your place among the saviors of the world

2:1-4	your weakness (identifying with your body)	the strength of Christ in you
3:1	a failure to learn the lesson, which brought pain	learning the lesson, which will bring escape from pain

Here is a version of "My brother, choose again," that incorporates all of the above:

> You chose before to identify with your weakness, your body, and thus to stay in hell and hold your brothers there. In doing so, you failed to learn the right lesson and so brought pain on yourself. My brother, choose again. Choose to learn the lesson, and escape all the pain that your previous choice brought to you. Choose to identify with the strength of Christ in you. In doing so you will take your place as a savior of the world, rescuing your brothers from hell.

5. The two appearances of Christ are different ways of describing the same appearance. In both, you are in a painful situation resulting from having made the wrong choice. In both, Christ comes to you. In both, He asks you to choose again. Here is a composite version of the two appearances:

> In every difficulty, all distress, and each perplexity – whenever you are feeling tried because you have chosen to identify with your weak and frail body – Christ comes to you. He appears to you in all His glory and gently says, "My brother, choose once again if you would take your place among the saviors of the world, or would remain in hell and hold your brothers there."

Chapter 8

Step II. Interpretation
B. Plugging in the Meaning of Terms, Phrases, and Pronouns

i. Terms and phrases

In this simple technique, you replace certain terms or phrases that you have identified in the observation step with their expanded meanings, to see what, if anything, this adds to your understanding of the sentence.

Example 1:

As we pointed out in Chapter 6, you might take the meaning of the word "temptation," as derived from its definition in T-30.VIII.3:1, and use that meaning to replace the word in T-31.VIII.1:1-2, perhaps rephrasing other parts of the sentences for clarity. Here is the original version from the Text:

> Temptation has one lesson it would teach, in all its forms, wherever it occurs. It would persuade the holy Son of God he is a body, born in what must die, unable to escape its frailty, and bound by what it orders him to feel. (T-31.VIII.1:1-2)

Now let's plug in the meaning of "temptation":

> *The wish to make illusions real,* in all its forms, wherever it occurs, is meant to teach the Son of God only one lesson: that he is a body....

From this substitution, you might realize that the main illusion that temptation is trying to reinforce is the illusion that we are bodies. By implication, then, anything that tends to reinforce our sense that the body is our reality is some form of temptation coming from our egos.

Example 2:

For another example, let's use T-31.VIII.4:2:

> Be never fearful of temptation, then, but see it as it is; another chance to choose again, and let Christ's strength prevail in every circumstance and every place you raised an image of yourself before.

Now let's plug in the meaning of "temptation" and of "image":

> Be never fearful of *the wish to make illusions real,* then, but see it as it is; another chance to choose again, and let Christ's strength prevail in every circumstance and every place you raised a *false picture* of yourself before.

Here the expanded meaning helps me to see that temptation is not something that comes from outside me; it is my own wish to make illusions real. Yet I need not be afraid of my twisted impulses. When they arise I can view them as a wonderful opportunity to choose differently – to see Christ as my reality, rather than the false self-concept I have made up. When my ego raises its head, it isn't a threat; it's an opportunity!

Example 3:

Expanding key terms in a sentence by replacing them with their definition can add to your understanding and avoid confusion. For instance, we need to avoid mistaken meanings for some of the Christian terms in the Course.

In T-31.VIII.4:3, the very next sentence in the Text, we see the phrase, "face of Christ." If we have observed this phrase and have researched its meaning a bit – perhaps looking it up in a glossary of Course terms and phrases – we will have found that it is a symbol of the holiness in ourselves and in all things, the holiness looked upon through true perception. We can substitute that more literal meaning into the sentence, and help uncover what it means:

> For what ["what" refers to those false images we make of ourselves] appears to hide *your holiness* is powerless before Christ's majesty, and disappears before His holy sight.

You may notice how this substitution complements and goes along with the one we made in the preceding sentence. The meaning of the whole paragraph begins to become more clear. We need not be afraid of our temptation to buy into false images of ourselves. Why? Because we can see this temptation as a chance to choose again, and because our false images are powerless before Christ's majesty. They may *appear* to hide His "face" in us, but they cannot really do so. Once we choose to overlook them, we will realize they were never there in the first place.

Example 4:

Sometimes the substitution does not involve any kind of

specialized terminology; it is simply a phrase the Course is using to summarize something that has been recently discussed. It can be very helpful to pause as you read and remind yourself what is being referred to by that summary phrase.

For instance, in "The Laws of Chaos" (T-23.II), five "laws" on which the ego's chaotic system depends are presented. When you reach paragraph 18, you read these words:

> You would maintain, and think it true, that you do not believe these senseless laws, nor act upon them. And when you look at what they say, they cannot be believed. Brother, you *do* believe them. (T-23.II.18:1-3)

This is a good time to remind ourselves what is meant by "these senseless laws." When Jesus says to us, "Brother, you *do* believe them," what laws are they he is telling us we believe, even though we profess, *with complete honesty, believing it is true,* that we do not believe them? This is referring to all five of the "laws" of chaos. We could expand on this meaning at length, using all five of the laws:

> I maintain, and think it true, that I do not believe that the truth is different for everyone [the first law of chaos, found in T-23.II.2:1], but I *do* believe that truth is different for everyone.

> I maintain, and think it true, that I do not believe that each one must sin, and therefore deserves attack and death (see T-23.II.4:1), but I *do* believe that.

And so on with the remaining three laws. Stopping along the way like this to fill in the meaning, so to speak, can bring the message of the Course home in a powerful way.

ii. Pronouns

Replacing pronouns with the nouns they refer to can be very powerful and very revealing. Often, meanings that were obscure will become quite plain.

Example 1:

Look again at T-31.VIII.1:2:

> It would persuade the holy Son of God he is a body, born in what must die, unable to escape its frailty, and bound by what it orders him to feel.

What do the various pronouns refer to? The first "it" refers to "temptation" (from 1:1). "He" refers to the holy Son of God (right before "he" in this same sentence). "Its" refers to the body. The second "it" also refers to the body. "Him" refers again to the holy Son of God, who is a limitless, spiritual being. (Both "he" and "him," as well as the phrase "holy Son of God," can also be understood to refer to "me.") Plugging in these meanings, the sentence reads as follows:

> Temptation would persuade the holy Son of God – me, a limitless spiritual being – that I am a body, born in what must die, unable to escape that body's frailty, and bound by what my body orders me to feel.

Do you see how simply replacing the pronouns with the nouns to which they refer can bring the message of that sentence home with a great deal of power?

Example 2:

One of our favorite examples for showing the clarity of understanding that can come simply by identifying the pronouns and replacing them with the nouns they refer to is in

T-18.IX.4. We will quote the whole paragraph below, and will highlight the pronouns with boldface type:

> The circle of fear lies just below the level the body sees, and seems to be the whole foundation on which the world is based. Here are all the illusions, all the twisted thoughts, all the insane attacks, the fury, the vengeance and betrayal that were made to keep the guilt in place, so that the world could rise from **it** and keep **it** hidden. **Its** shadow rises to the surface, enough to hold **its** most external manifestations in darkness, and to bring despair and loneliness to **it** and keep **it** joyless. Yet **its** intensity is veiled by its heavy coverings, and kept apart from **what** was made to keep **it** hidden. The body cannot see **this,** for the body arose from **this** for **its** protection, which depends on keeping **it** not seen. The body's eyes will never look on **it**. Yet **they** will see what **it** dictates. (T-18.IX.4:1-7)

As you read that, don't you find yourself getting lost in regard to what "it," "its," "what," and "this" refer to? Going through and trying to identify what each pronoun refers to makes the whole paragraph much clearer. First of all, the paragraph begins by talking about a "circle of fear" that resides "just below" everything seen by the body's eyes. This refers to an invisible layer of fear underlying the visible world. In this circle of fear are all the attack thoughts that *seem to be* the foundation on which the world is based (4:1). And yet, as the paragraph goes on, we see that is not the whole picture.

All of these things belonging to the circle of fear "were made to keep the guilt in place." The picture here is of another, hidden layer, beneath the fear. This third layer consists of guilt. The fear somehow separates this layer of guilt from the surface world, and though the world seems to be founded on that layer of fear, in reality the world is rising from "it" (the guilt) and at the same time helping to keep "it" (the guilt) hidden. Let's rephrase the next few sentences, substituting "guilt" for "it" where appropriate, and other words when they are appropriate:

> Here are all the illusions, all the twisted thoughts, all the insane attacks, the fury, the vengeance and betrayal that were made to keep the guilt in place, so that the world could rise from **that guilt** and keep **that guilt** hidden. **Guilt's** shadow rises to the surface, enough to hold **guilt's** most external manifestations [the physical world] in darkness, and to bring despair and loneliness to **the world** and keep the **world joyless.** Yet **guilt's** intensity is veiled by **guilt's** heavy coverings ["coverings" plural, a reference to both the circle of fear and to the world], and kept apart from **the world which** was made to keep **guilt** hidden. The body cannot see **this guilt,** for the body arose from **the guilt** for **guilt's** protection, which depends on keeping **the guilt** not seen. The body's eyes will never look on **the guilt.** Yet **the body's eyes** will see what **guilt** dictates.

Although this paragraph still presents a rather complex picture of three layers, all of which interact and relate to one another, tracking down the pronouns has at least begun to bring a measure of clarity. Though the word "guilt" actually occurs only once in the paragraph, nearly the entire paragraph is about guilt. The world arises from guilt, and yet is made in order to hide the guilt that gives birth to the world.

The body is part of the visible world and therefore shares the world's purpose – to keep guilt unseen and hidden. Therefore, the body will never see the guilt; its purpose is to keep the guilt unseen.

We did not, however, merely plug in "guilt" wherever we saw a pronoun. One sentence in particular required some careful work, the sentence beginning with "Its [guilt's] shadow rises to the surface." At first glance, it would appear that all the "its" in the sentence refer to guilt (grammatically, this would make the most sense). This works for the first two "its," but for the last two "its" this would make no logical sense. So then we tried searching for other nouns that might fit. We saw "external manifestations" and wondered if the last two "its" refer to this. We would normally rule this out, however, because if the last two pronouns refer to "external manifestations" (a plural), then grammatically speaking, they ought to be plural pronouns: "...bring despair and loneliness to them and keep them joyless."

We finally settled upon "world," based on the recognition that "external manifestations" is just another way of saying "world" (and also based on the fact that "world" is mentioned in the previous sentence). In essence, we replaced "external manifestations" with "world," and thus "world" became the immediately preceding noun to which the final two "its" refer.

We then reread the passage with "world" replacing the final two "its" and discovered that it made sense – the passage came together, everything fit. This shows that we picked the correct noun. This highlights an important principle of Course interpretation: "If there is a conflict between grammatical sense and logical sense in a passage, logical sense overrules grammatical sense."[1]

As you can see from this example, it is not always easy to identify these pronouns. Is there a method for doing so? Unfortunately, there is no easy method that we are aware of. The following two-step process is the one we use:

1. Try out the noun that immediately precedes (and grammatically fits) the pronoun.

This works most of the time. For instance: "No one who would unite in any way with anyone for his individual salvation will find it in that strange relationship" (T-13.X.2:9). Here, it is obvious that "it" refers to "salvation," the noun that immediately precedes it.

2. If the first step yields poor results, try out other nearby nouns to see which one makes sense in that sentence and brings meaning and unity to the passage as a whole.

Unfortunately, the first step often doesn't work. When you try the first step and its results make no sense, it is time to go hunting. Identify other logical nouns in the vicinity and try them out. Put one of these nouns in place of the pronoun and see if the sentence makes sense. Then read the other sentences around this sentence and see if the passage as a whole now makes sense. If you have selected the right noun, the entire passage will often take on surprising meaning and unity. All the pieces will fit together and add up to a single overall idea. The whole thing will have a single thrust. When you see all the pieces fall together, when everything fits, that is when you know you have the right noun.

Let's look at a few examples of this second step:

---

[1] We are indebted to Greg Mackie for coining this rule.

Example 3:

> No real relationship can rest on guilt, or even hold one spot of it to mar its purity. (T-13.X.2:2)

"It" would normally refer to "guilt," and in this case it does; the sentence makes sense when read that way. We might also expect "its" to refer to guilt, but it cannot. How can we speak of "guilt's purity"? That's ridiculous. So we have to hunt for a better candidate. The nearest candidate is "real relationship." Let's try that out:

> No real relationship can rest on **guilt,** or even hold one spot of guilt to mar **the real relationship's** purity.

This, we can readily see, makes sense. Now both parts of the sentence express the same idea: A real relationship can contain no guilt. Also, speaking of the purity of a real (or holy) relationship makes sense, just as speaking of the purity of guilt did not.

Example 4:

> Fear not to recognize the whole idea of sacrifice as solely of your making. And seek not safety by attempting to protect yourself from where it is not. (T-15.XI.1:1-2)

What does the "it" refer to here? "Safety" is the nearest noun, but it is not the best fit. Let's try it in the sentence and see: "And seek not safety by attempting to protect yourself from where safety is not." This isn't nonsense. If someone gave us this sentence and told us it was from the Course, we might think it means this: "Seek not safety by trying to protect yourself from a dangerous world (rather, realize that danger is not real)."

The problem with this is that it ignores the connection between this sentence and the previous one. The two sentences begin in a parallel fashion: "fear not"..."seek not." This suggests they are both about the same thing. The first is about sacrifice, or rather, the self-made nature of sacrifice. Thus, the second sentence probably is, too. Let's put "sacrifice" in place of "it" and see if it works:

> Fear not to recognize the whole idea of sacrifice as solely of your making. And seek not safety by attempting to protect yourself from where **sacrifice** is not.

Now the passage makes sense. It all falls together and its meaning becomes clear: "Don't be afraid to see that sacrifice is just an idea that you made up. And don't seek safety by trying to protect yourself from the sacrifice you perceive as demanded of you (by your brothers and your Father, who are mentioned in the next sentence), since that is not where sacrifice is. The demand for sacrifice is in *you*."

In this case, if you read the sentence by itself you would be quite justified in seeing "it" as referring to "safety," yet this turns out to be wrong. You have to read the previous sentence and realize that both sentences are talking about the same thing. Only then do you see that "it" must refer to "sacrifice." Bringing a unified meaning to the passage as a whole is key to the proper identification of pronouns.

Exercise in plugging in the meaning of terms, phrases, and pronouns

For this exercise we will again use Paragraph 3 from "Choose Once Again":

> 1. Trials are but lessons that you failed to learn pre-

sented once again, so where you made a faulty choice before you now can make a better one, and thus escape all pain that what you chose before has brought to you. 2. In every difficulty, all distress, and each perplexity Christ calls to you and gently says, "My brother, choose again." 3. He would not leave one source of pain unhealed, nor any image left to veil the truth. 4. He would remove all misery from you whom God created altar unto joy. 5. He would not leave you comfortless, alone in dreams of hell, but would release your mind from everything that hides His face from you. 6. His holiness is yours because He is the only Power that is real in you. 7. His strength is yours because He is the Self That God created as His only Son. (T-31.VIII.3)

1. In Sentences 3-6 there are several masculine pronouns. Who do they refer to? **2.** To Whom does the final "His" in Sentence 7 refer to?

3. Sentence 2: "difficulty, distress and perplexity" refer to a difficult, distressing or perplexing situation. What other word in this paragraph expresses this same idea?

4. Sentence 2: "Christ." Can you find a definition of this term elsewhere in this paragraph?

5. Sentence 3: What is the "source of pain," based strictly on this paragraph? Look for other occurrences of the word "pain."

6. Sentence 5: "hell." This word has a recent word history which supplies its meaning here. The previous section contained several references to hell. Here is one: "At least, you merely look on darkness, and perceive the terrified imaginings that come from guilty thoughts and concepts born of fear. And what you see is hell, for fear *is* hell" (T-31.VII.7:5-6). Based on this passage, what does "hell" mean in our current sentence? Is it an afterlife condition or our current condition?

7. Sentence 5: "everything that hides His face from you." What in this paragraph hides His face from you? Look for something else that is described as hiding something good and true from your awareness.

ANSWER KEY

1. Christ

2. God

3. Trials

4. Sentence 7: "He is the Self That God created as His only Son." Since you and everyone else are Sons of God, this phrase means that Christ is the one Self shared by you and everyone else.

5. "What you chose before" (Sentence 1), which brought you pain. The source of pain is your faulty choice which caused you to fail to learn the lesson.

6. "Hell" here means not an afterlife condition, but our current condition. The passage quoted talks about hell as the fear that we feel, given the world that we perceive.

7. Sentence 3 refers to images (false images of yourself) that veil the truth. These are what hide Christ's face from you. Note that a veil is a covering for a face.

Here is a reworded version of Paragraph 3 which contains all of the information we have gained thus far about the meaning of its terms, phrases and pronouns:

1. Trials are but lessons that you failed to learn presented once again, so where you made a faulty choice before you now can make a better one, and thus escape all pain that your previous faulty choice brought to you. 2. In every trial, Christ, your true Self, calls to you and gently says, "My brother, choose again." 3. Christ would not leave unhealed a single pain-producing faulty choice, nor any false image of yourself left to veil the truth. 4. Christ would remove all misery from you whom God created altar unto joy. 5. Christ would not leave you comfortless, alone in your dreams of a fearful, hellish world, but would release your mind from all the false images of yourself that hide Christ's face from you. 6. Christ's holiness is yours because He is the only Power that is real in you. 7. Christ's strength is yours because He is your Self, the Self That God created as God's only Son.

Chapter 9

Step II. Interpretation
C. Getting the Meaning of the Sentence

The idea here is making sure you really understand each sentence before you move beyond it. We're not suggesting that you need to perform this step for every sentence in the Course. We do suggest that you use it with every sentence whose meaning seems unclear to you.

i. Reduce the sentence to its basic gist or essence

Finding the subject, verb and object helps you do this. Usually it involves, at the start, leaving out modifiers and qualifiers, and then adding them in bit by bit. If you are familiar with the old grammatic practice of diagramming sentences, that can be helpful here. It can mean rewording the sentence, putting it into your own words. It can also mean lumping several specifics into a general term (see fourth example below).

Example 1:

> Forgiveness recognizes what you thought your brother did to you has not occurred. (W-pII.1.1:1)

The gist of the sentence is, "Forgiveness recognizes." The rest of the sentence defines what is recognized.

Example 2:

> Choose once again if you would take your place among the saviors of the world, or would remain in hell, and hold your brothers there. (T-31.VIII.1:5)

The gist is: Choose if you would be a savior or remain in hell.

Example 3:

> Simply by never using weakness to direct your actions, you have given it no power. (T-31.VIII.2:5)

In other words: You give no power to weakness when you don't follow its directions.

Example 4:

> What you behold as sickness and as pain, as weakness and as suffering and loss, is but temptation to perceive yourself defenseless and in hell. (T-31.VIII.6:2)

Gist, paraphrase: Seeing others as suffering is only the temptation to see yourself as a victim.

ii. Reword the sentence to express this gist

We have done this in the examples above. It isn't always necessary to complete this step; sometimes just getting a general sense of the meaning is enough. If you want to be certain you have the meaning, try rewording the sentence, putting it into your own words, either mentally or by writing it down. Let's take a sentence and give several rewordings, each of which captures a slightly different aspect of meaning. Here is the original sentence from the Course:

> You always choose between your weakness and the strength of Christ in you. (T-31.VIII.2:3)

Now, three ways of rewording the sentence:

> Every choice is one between the ego and Christ.

> To identify with my separate self is to choose weakness, to identify with Christ is to choose strength.

> My choice is always between my weak images of myself and the strength of who I am in Christ.

iii. Let related ideas come to help the meaning sink in

Related ideas are ones suggested by the original idea, but not overtly included in the wording.

Example:

Continuing with the above short sentence, some related ideas might be:

> Alone I am weak; in Christ I am strong.

> I have the strength of Christ in me to use whenever I choose to.

> The ego's thoughts always disempower me; my reality always empowers me.

> I am strong when I identify with the eternal Son of God in me.

> In the situation regarding ____, I choose to trust the strength of Christ in me.

> I will not trust my own weakness in this situation.

For other examples of "related thoughts," see Workbook Lessons 81 to 90, where the sentences in italics are thoughts related to the main lesson ideas. Many Workbook lessons (beginning with Lessons 39 and 42) are designed to teach us how to come up with related thoughts; some skill at doing this seems to be an important part of the curriculum. Allowing related thoughts to come makes the original statements sink more deeply into our minds. It makes them more fully our own. In this way, God's Thoughts become our thoughts. This practice literally trains our mind in thinking God's Thoughts along with Him.

Exercise in getting the meaning of the sentence

We will again use Paragraph 3 from "Choose Once Again":

> 1. Trials are but lessons that you failed to learn presented once again, so where you made a faulty choice before you now can make a better one, and thus escape all pain that what you chose before has brought to you. 2. In every difficulty, all distress, and each perplexity Christ calls to you and gently says, "My brother, choose again." 3. He would not leave one source of pain unhealed, nor any image left to veil the truth. 4. He would remove all misery from you whom God created altar unto joy. 5. He would not leave you comfortless, alone in dreams of hell, but would release your mind from everything that hides His face from you. 6. His holiness is yours because He is the only Power that is real in you. 7. His strength is yours because He is the Self That God created as His only Son. (T-31.VIII.3)

1. Try rewording Sentence 1 to express the gist of it.

2. Let some thoughts related to Sentence 1 come to you. Look at the sentence, relax your mind, and let thoughts come that relate to its themes.

3. Reduce Sentence 2 to its basic gist or essence. Try to use as few words as possible.

4. Let some thoughts related to Sentence 7 come. Remember that you are God's Son and so Christ is your Self.

ANSWER KEY

1. Here are some possible rewordings of Sentence 1:

Trials are unlearned lessons presented again so that now you can learn them.

Trials are lessons you chose to not learn presented again so that now I can make a different choice.

A trial is an opportunity to choose again and escape the pain a previous poor choice brought to you.

2. Some thoughts related to Sentence 1:

If I make a better choice in each trial I experience, I will be free.

If I learn to choose correctly, I will escape all pain.

Christ will always give me another chance to learn.

3. In every trial Christ asks you to choose again.

4. Some thoughts related to Sentence 7:

    Christ's strength is mine because He is my Self.
    I am God's Son. Everything He has is mine.
    Christ's strength is unlimited and His strength is mine.
    God created me and so my nature must reflect His.

Chapter 10

Step II. Interpretation
D. Following the Logic

Logic is an activity whereby conclusions are proven because they follow logically from premises which are assumed or accepted. If the premises are true, and if the conclusions logically follow from the premises, then the conclusions must also be true.

The Course frequently uses logical argument, and sometimes even states things in the form of a classic logical syllogism (that is, "If A is true, and B is true, then C must also be true." For instance, "An animal that eats only vegetable matter is called a herbivore. All cows eat only vegetable matter. Therefore, cows are herbivores."). This frequent use of logic is natural, for the Course's purpose is to change minds and logic is an ancient tool of mental change, one that we use every day.

The purpose of being aware of the Course's use of logic is

to allow that logic to work its effect on our minds to the fullest possible extent. Following the Course's logic allows its idea to sink more deeply into our minds and become strengthened within us.

"Now take this personally"

Here is an example of Jesus using logic to persuade Helen Schucman's mind. This is personal guidance to Helen recorded in Ken Wapnick's *Absence from Felicity*:

> Now take this personally, and listen to Divine logic: If, when you have been forgiven, you have everything else, and *if you have been forgiven,* then you *have* everything else.
>
> This happens to be the simplest of all propositions.
> If P then Q.
> P.
> Therefore, Q.
>
> The real question is, is P true? If you will review the evidence, I think you will find this inescapable. I went on very personal record to this effect, and I am the only completely true Witness for God. You have every right to examine my credentials – in fact, I urge you to do so. You haven't read the Bible in years.
>
> (*Absence from Felicity,* p. 229)

This material gives us a number of clues as to how we should treat the Course's logic. First, he calls it "Divine logic." Imagine that! Logic can actually be Divine. The Course itself mentions the same idea: "The Holy Spirit uses logic as easily and as well as does the ego, except that His conclusions are not insane" (T-14.IN.1:4).

Second, notice how much Jesus encourages Helen to ponder the premise. The logic in this argument is so simple that the only real issue is: Is the premise true? If the premise is true, then the conclusion is also. Jesus therefore urges Helen to consider the evidence for this premise. He says that he went on "very personal record" on behalf of this premise (the idea that we have been forgiven). Therefore, accepting this premise is largely a matter of trusting him. Helen is thus encouraged to read the Bible and examine Jesus' credentials, to see if she can take his word in this matter.

Finally, he urges Helen to take the whole thing personally. Taking something personally often means internalizing something insulting or humiliating. Here, it means internalizing something liberating. Jesus wants us to apply the conclusions of his logic quite personally to ourselves. His logic is not meant to remain a series of abstract propositions. It is meant to transform how we look at ourselves.

The spiritual practice of reflecting on logic

We often think of logic and spiritual practice as being antithetical. We think of true spiritual practice as going beyond words and reason to a state that transcends them both. Yet, in the Course, spiritual practice is a means of changing our minds. Logic is also a means of changing our minds. They both have the same purpose. And, as the Course says, "What shares a common purpose is the same. This is the law of purpose" (T-27.VI.1:5-6). In the Course, then, it is quite natural to combine logic and spiritual practice. This is exactly what happens in Lesson 66. There, we spend ten to fifteen minutes reflecting on a logical syllogism. This exercise reveals so much about the Course's use of logic that we would like to comment on it at some length:

> Begin the ten-to-fifteen-minute practice period by reviewing these thoughts:
>
> *God gives me only happiness.*
> *He has given my function to me.*
> *Therefore my function must be happiness.*
>
> Try to see the logic in this sequence, even if you do not yet accept the conclusion. It is only if the first two thoughts are wrong that the conclusion could be false. Let us, then, think about the premises for a while, as we are practicing. (W-pI.66.5)

Here we are given a classic Aristotelian syllogism, consisting of two premises and a conclusion. For ten to fifteen minutes we are supposed to simply review this syllogism. We are given two ways in which to review it. First, try to see the logic in it; see that the conclusion does logically follow from the two premises. Second, think about the premises; see if we can accept them. For it is only if they are wrong that the conclusion can be false.

The next paragraphs then guide us through a process of reviewing the two premises. Let's see how they do that:

> The first premise is that God gives you only happiness. This could be false, of course, but in order to be false it is necessary to define God as something He is

> not. Love cannot give evil, and what is not happiness is evil. God cannot give what He does not have, and He cannot have what He is not. Unless God gives you only happiness, He must be evil. And it is this definition of Him you are believing if you do not accept the first premise. (W-pI.66.6)

This paragraph is an example of the kind of reflection we are supposed to do during the exercise. It is an extended consideration of the first premise. Its logic is quite compelling. It links giving, having, and being in a causal chain. It says that God can only *give* what He *has*, and can only *have* what He *is*. It also says that what is not happiness is evil. Thus, if God is giving you something besides happiness, He is giving you evil. And if He *gives* evil, then He must *have* evil; and if He *has* evil, then He must *be* evil. "And it is this definition of Him you are believing if you do not accept the first premise."

In other words, if you want to reject this first premise, you must be willing to assert that God is evil. Are you willing to go that far? If not, then accepting the first premise is your only option.

> The second premise is that God has given you your function. We have seen that there are only two parts of your mind. One is ruled by the ego, and is made up of illusions. The other is the home of the Holy Spirit, where truth abides. There are no other guides but these to choose between, and no other outcomes possible as a result of your choice but the fear that the ego always engenders, and the love that the Holy Spirit always offers to replace it.

> Thus, it must be that your function is established by God through His Voice, or is made by the ego which you have made to replace Him. Which is true? Unless God gave your function to you, it must be the gift of the ego. Does the ego really have gifts to give, being itself an illusion and offering only the illusion of gifts?
> (W-pI.66.7-8)

These two paragraphs are a consideration of the second premise, that God has given you your function, the role you are supposed to play in the greater whole. Again, this consideration presents you with a stark either/or choice. Either God has given you your function, or the ego has. There are only these two parts of your mind. There are only these two guides to follow in your life. But how can the ego give you your function? The idea of giving gifts implies some real agent giving you some real thing. Yet the ego is only an illusion. Therefore, all it can give is an *illusion* of a gift. The ego cannot, therefore, give you your function. Only God can.

> Think about this during the longer practice period today. Think also about the many forms the illusion of your function has taken in your mind, and the many ways in which you tried to find salvation under the ego's guidance. Did you find it? Were you happy? Did they bring you peace? We need great honesty today. Remember the outcomes fairly, and consider also whether it was ever reasonable to expect happiness from anything the ego ever proposed. Yet the ego is the only alternative to the Holy Spirit's Voice. (W-pI.66.9)

This paragraph begins by reaffirming that the previous two

paragraphs are there to guide your reflection during the exercise. It then goes on to offer further guidance. It asks you to reflect on the illusions of your function that your ego has given you, and ask yourself if they have made you happy. In other words, you are being asked to reflect on the fact that your life thus far has expressed a different syllogism, which we might put in this way:

> *My ego has given me many functions.*
> *Nothing my ego has given me has brought happiness.*
> *My ego-given functions have not brought me happiness.*

Considering that your life has reflected an alternate syllogism has, we think, a fairly obvious purpose. It motivates you to accept the Course's new syllogism. When you realize that the roles (or functions) you have played in your life have not delivered the fulfillment they promised, you will desire an alternative scenario. You will *want* to believe that God is offering you a new role. You will *want* to believe that what He gives will bring you happiness.

> You will listen to madness or hear the truth. Try to make this choice as you think about the premises on which our conclusion rests. We can share in this conclusion, but in no other. For God Himself shares it with us. (W-pI.66.10)

This last paragraph reveals the point of the whole exercise. It says that this is an exercise in choosing to hear the truth rather than listen to madness. This means, more specifically, it is an exercise in choosing to turn to God for our function rather than to the ego. The logic is meant to persuade us that choosing God's function for us is smarter than choosing the ego's. It will make us happy, while the ego has failed to do. Being thus persuaded, we will hopefully go ahead and make that choice.

Guidelines for making use of the Course's logic

The above passages – from Helen's personal guidance and from Lesson 66 – provide a window onto how to approach the Course's logic. Notice how parallel they are. Both use logic to effect a practical change in our thinking. Both ask us to reflect on the truth of the premises. Based on the above two examples, we recommend the following guidelines for making use of the Course's logic:

- Look for the use of logic in the Course. Look for any situation in which one idea is supported or justified by other ideas. Look for the following key words: "for," "because," "therefore," "if," "then," and "thus."
- Identify the premise or premises. Premises are the rationale, support, or justification for the conclusion. However, they often are given after the conclusion. Look for words like "for," "because," or "if."
- Identify the conclusion. The conclusion is the idea the author is trying to prove or support. It is the point, the punch line. Look for words like "therefore," "then," or "thus."
- Ask yourself, "Does the conclusion follow from the premise(s)?" Is the argument logical?
- See if you can accept the premise(s). This, as we said, was the main emphasis in the two examples of logic we looked at.

- Take the conclusion personally. Let it in and see what practical changes it causes in your mind.

Other examples:

First, a classic logical syllogism:

> The Christ in you inhabits not a body. Yet He is in you. And thus it must be that you are not within a body. What is within you cannot be outside. And it is certain that you cannot be apart from what is at the very center of your life. (T-25.IN.11-5)

The basic syllogism is in the first three sentences; the remaining two sentences offer supporting logic for the premises. The premises are 1) Christ does not inhabit a body, and 2) Christ is in you. The conclusion is, "you are not within a body." If the premises are true, the conclusion must also be true. Notice your reactions to the idea that you are not within a body.

Second, a more general logical argument, a kind which abounds in the Course:

> They [the saviors of the world] will redeem the world, for they are joined in all the power of the Will of God. (T-31.VIII.4:4)

In this sentence the word "for" is a clue that some kind of logic is being used. What is the premise? Here, it is that the saviors of the world are joined in all the power of the Will of God. What is the conclusion? That these saviors will redeem the world. Does the conclusion follow from the premise? If they had all that power, would they be able to redeem the world? It certainly seems reasonable to think so. The crucial question, then, is, "Can I accept the premise?" Here we need to think it through. If God would not give his power to those dedicated to saving the world, it would mean that He does not want to save it; He would be an uncaring God. If, therefore, you believe that God is loving and wants the world to be saved, then you can accept the premise that He would give all of His power to these saviors. Finally, we can think how accepting the conclusion makes us feel, what the implications are. The age-old quest to save the world is not futile. It is guaranteed to succeed.

Exercise in following the logic

We will again use Paragraph 3 from "Choose Once Again." This time we will focus only on those sentences that make use of logic.

1. Sentence 4. "He would remove all misery from you whom God created altar unto joy." The use of logic in this sentence is clearer if we rephrase it: "He would remove all misery from you, for God created you as an altar unto joy." We have two parts to this sentence. One is the premise and the other is the conclusion. Which is which? Remember, the premise provides the rationale for the conclusion.

2. Sentence 6. "His holiness is yours because He is the only Power that is real in you." Note: "Because" is usually a give-away that logic is being used. A conclusion is said to be true "because" of a certain premise. So the phrase following "because" is the premise and the phrase preceding "because" is the conclusion. Using this information, try writing out a logical syllogism based on the above sentence, following this form:

First premise:

Second premise (an unstated premise needed to connect the first premise to the conclusion):

Conclusion:

3. Sentence 7. "His strength is yours because He is the Self That God created as His only Son." Note the word "because" again. Remember that the conclusion is true *because* of the premise. Again, identify the premise and the conclusion.

ANSWER KEY

1. The premise is: God created you altar unto joy; God created you joyous. The conclusion is: He (Christ) would remove all misery from you. There seems to be an unstated premise here (this is often the case in the Course): Christ would remove everything that does not reflect how you were created. Based on this, we can construct the following syllogism:

Christ would remove everything that does not reflect the condition in which you were created.
God created you joyous.
Therefore, Christ would remove everything from you that is not joyous.

Now apply to this syllogism the guidelines we suggested. First, ask yourself if the logic is valid. Does the conclusion follow logically from the two premises?

Second, reflect on the truth of the premises (the first two statements).

Premise #1: Do you think that Christ (your true Self) would want to remove from you everything that does not reflect how you were created? Do you think your true Self would want to remove anything that does not reflect your true nature?

Premise #2: Do you think that God created you joyous? If not, what does that say about God?

If you think the logic is valid, and you can accept the two premises, realize that for you the conclusion is proven. Your true Self wants to remove everything from you that is not joyous. Let this conclusion in. You might want to let some related thoughts come, such as: "My Self wants only my happiness"; "He only wants to take away my pain."

2. *Christ is the only Power that is really in you.*
Christ is holy.
Christ's holiness is in you; His holiness is yours.

Again, do you think the conclusion follows logically from the premises? If Christ is the only thing real in you, and if Christ is holy, would His holiness be yours?

Can you accept the premises? Can you accept that your true Self is the only thing that is real in you? Can you accept that your true Self is holy?

If the argument is logical and if you can accept the premises, then let the conclusion sink in. Take it personally.

3. The premise: Christ is the Self God created as God's only Son.
The conclusion: Christ's strength is yours.

We think that there are two unstated premises in this logical argument. The sentence assumes, but does not say, that Christ is strong and that you are God's Son. Adding in these unstated premises, we can construct two syllogisms:

Christ is the Self that God created as His Son.
You are God's Son.
Christ is your Self.

Christ is your Self. All He has is yours.
Christ is strong.
Christ's strength is yours.

Again, do you think the logic follows in these two syllogisms? Can you accept the premises? Note that in the second syllogism, the first premise has already been established, being the conclusion of the previous syllogism. If you think the logic follows and if you can accept the premises, then the conclusion has been proven for you. Let it sink in. Take it personally. Let some related thoughts come to fill out its meaning for you.

Chapter 11

Step 11. Interpretation
E. Recognizing When Passages Address Specific Situations, Issues or Beliefs

Quite often, the Course is speaking directly to a specific situation, issue or conventional belief. Usually, identifying this specific thing is an enormous help in understanding and applying the message of the passage. Without knowing the context which the passage is addressing, its dictums and observations may seem little more than a random set of disconnected principles. Yet when you identify the central situation or issue that the passage is attempting to deal with, suddenly it comes alive. It becomes a vibrant, unified whole, with real, down-to-earth implications in your life.

i. Personal circumstances of the scribes

There are several variations of this same theme in the Course. For instance, many passages, particularly in the Text, gain added meaning when the reader recognizes that, in the original dictation as given to Helen Schucman, many of the words applied to specific situations in her life, or in Bill Thetford's life. Obviously, to know the details of Helen's and Bill's lives requires outside reading. Both *Journey Without Distance* by Robert Skutch and *Absence From Felicity* by Kenneth Wapnick tell the story of the scribing of the Course and give some details. Wapnick's book is the most helpful in identifying specific incidents in the lives of the scribes that resulted in passages later included in the Course.

For instance, consider the famous prayer in Chapter Two of the Text: "I am here only to be truly helpful..."(T-2.V.18:2-6). This prayer is certainly moving and meaningful in its own right. However, *Absence from Felicity* tells us that the prayer was originally given to Bill specifically to encourage him to attend a professional conference on rehabilitation that he was not keen on attending. This shows us that the Holy Spirit does, indeed, take an interest in the healing potential even of our professional lives. This is a prayer, not just for use when we engage in what we might normally think of as "service work," but also for taking part in our daily job.

There are scores of such instances in the Course. Many can be detected even without detailed reading outside the Course itself, simply by bearing in mind that the material was originally given to Helen and Bill for the healing of their own personal relationship, and that the holy relationship referred to in the Text was, in the primary case, that relationship. In fact, one of the main specific situations referred to in the Course is their original moment of joining, when Bill said "there must be a better way," and Helen agreed to help him find it. This is referred to dozens of times in the Text (in Chapters 17-22). A requirement for understanding those chapters is simply being able to spot all of the ways in which that event is referred to. Here are some examples:

> You undertook, together, to invite the Holy Spirit into your relationship. (T-17.V.11:1)
>
> When you accepted the goal of truth as the goal of your relationship... (T-17.VIII.6:1)
>
> The holy instant in which you and your brother united... (T-18.IX.13:3)

ii. Conventional situations or issues

Often, the Course makes references, sometimes clear and sometimes subtle, to certain conventional situations or issues. For instance, in certain places the Course plainly speaks out about therapists and theologians. Some examples can be seen in T-9.V, "The Unhealed Healer."

Other instances can be seen in the Manual for Teachers. Many of its sections are speaking to a particular type of situation that the teacher of God will typically encounter. For instance, Section 7, "Should Healing Be Repeated?" addresses what to do when you have given healing to someone but no manifest physical change results. "Is Reincarnation So?" (M-24), deals with what to do when a pupil brings up tangential spiritual issues, such as the issue of reincarnation. Being clear on the main issue addressed in these sections transforms them from a collection of abstract statements into specific counsel for one's life.

Another example is the Text section titled, "The Immediacy of Salvation" (T-26.VIII). As you begin to read this section it is important to identify the situation it is dealing with, which is this: You have forgiven a brother, and are waiting for him to return your gift in some form. That situation is sketched for us in the first sentence of the section. If we do not pause and let that situation register in our minds, the rest of the section will lose nearly all of its impact. If we do realize what it is talking about, and go further to think of a similar situation in our own lives in which we are looking for some appropriate response to our forgiveness, the lines of the section not only become meaningful, but personally relevant.

Sometimes the issue is not immediately obvious. For instance, in Chapter 14 we read the following:

> If you believe you understand something of the "dynamics" of the ego, let me assure you that you understand nothing of it. For of yourself you could not understand it. The study of the ego is not the study of the mind. In fact, the ego enjoys studying itself, and thoroughly approves the undertakings of students who would "analyze" it, thus approving its importance. Yet they but study form with meaningless content. For their teacher is senseless, though careful to conceal this fact behind impressive sounding words, but which lack any consistent sense when they are put together.
>
> (T-14.X.8:4–9)

At first glance, this passage seems to be talking in general about the "dynamics" of the ego, which is a topic we might expect the Course to discuss in its own terms. A closer reading, however, leads us to believe that in this passage, the author has something quite specific in mind.

In the first place, it mentions a lot of specifics that suggest some concrete situation. Here we have studying, analyzing, teachers, students, and "impressive sounding words." The word "analyze" appears in quotes, which implies that the Course is referring to some particular (perhaps specialized) usage of that word. All these specifics should alert our minds to ask, "Is the Course referring to some specific context here, in which students speak of analyzing the ego?"

What else is said about the context?

- It seeks to understand the ego's dynamics.
- It claims to study the mind but actually only studies the ego.
- It has students and teachers.
- It analyzes the ego.
- It uses impressive sounding words.
- It has an intellectual bent, in view of words like "study," "understand," "students," and "teacher."

If we boil this down a bit, we see that the passage is talking about some intellectual context where students and teachers try to study the mind and analyze the ego. Is this starting to ring a bell, and sound like something you are familiar with?

Of course! It is referring to modern psychology. Once we deduce that, other aspects of the passage take on expanded meaning. The very word "psychology," for instance, means, "study of the mind." Also, the passage begins by referring to "you" thinking you understand ego dynamics. This might not be true of you as you read the passage, but it certainly was true of Helen and Bill as they first read it. By profession, they were psychologists engaged in an attempt to understand ego dynamics! (Incidentally, this is another instance of personal circumstances of the scribes, discussed in the last point. Sometimes the categories overlap.)

We can also now see that the "impressive sounding words" must refer to psychological jargon, which has become so esoteric and removed from common understanding that it is often referred to as "psychobabble."

Lastly, the word "analyze," in this context, almost certainly refers not simply to a general, systematic attempt to understand something, but quite specifically to Freudian analysis.

As soon as we realize that this passage is addressing the subject of modern psychology, we can apply its comments. And the commentary it makes is a devastating one:

- It says that modern psychology can never achieve its goal. Why? Because the human mind is unable to understand the ego within itself. Later paragraphs in the section will clarify that, by ourselves, we are within the ego's system. Looking at the ego from inside its own system, we cannot truly see that the ego is nothing. Only when we join minds is the nothingness of the ego revealed to us.
- It says that psychology does not study the mind, but only the ego. Since psychology means "study of the mind," modern psychology is not truly psychology!
- It says that the activity of studying the ego, and of analyzing it on the couch, is an act that approves of the ego's importance. The whole enterprise actually ends up feeding the ego.
- It implies that the ego is actually the teacher, the guiding presence behind modern psychology, and that all psycholo-

gists are the ego's eager students. If they are studying the ego, they must be the ego's students.

- It says that in studying the ego, psychology is really studying nothing. It studies form that has chaotic, senseless, empty content, because the ego itself is nothing.
- It says that psychological jargon is actually an attempt to hide this underlying lack of content. It uses involved, fancy form (words) to substitute for and draw attention away from empty content. In other words, psychology's big words mask the fact that behind those words is total nonsense (which reflects the non-sense that psychology studies, the ego).

That's a pretty shocking list, isn't it? Yet, if you had not realized that this passage was dealing with a particular, specific issue, and taken the time to identify that issue, the impact of the passage would have been minimal.

Doing the detective work

When you encounter a discussion in the Course that seems general and vague, perhaps you can uncover its underlying context. Here are some suggestions for identifying what specific thing or situation a passage is referring to. It is the procedure we followed above, made general and summed up:

1. *Realize that this passage refers to a specific situation or issue.*
First, you must catch on that this passage is talking about something specific in life. Just learn to be on the lookout for this in the Course. As we did above, notice some of the specific things mentioned in the passage, and try to see what they might apply to.

2. *Collect the clues in the passage that refer to the situation being addressed.*

The specifics just referred to are clues to the situation or issue being addressed. Mentally identify these and collect them in your mind.

3. *Identify the overall pattern produced by all these clues.*

Put the clues together into a single picture and overall pattern. In the preceding example, we did this in the paragraph that began with the words, "If we boil this down...."

4. *Search your mind for a situation or issue in normal life that fits this pattern.*

Once you find something in normal life that seems to fit the pattern, test it against the specifics to see if you have a real fit.

Of course, these steps are not strictly sequential. They occur simultaneously and affect one another. For instance, once you pull some clues together, you may get a hunch about what situation this is referring to. That hunch, then, can help you identify other clues, as well as see the pattern behind them. The main thing to remember here is, think about the passages you are reading. They are not just pretty words. What do they refer to? What do they apply to?

iii. The state of mind of the reader

Very, very often, the "context" that is being referred to by the Course, both in the Text and in the Workbook, is the reader's own state of mind. Jesus, the author, sometimes seems to be reading our minds as he anticipates and addresses our psychological reactions to what he is saying. For instance, he says:

> You are very new in the ways of salvation, and think you have lost your way. Your way is lost, but think not this is loss. (T-17.V.9:1–2)

As we begin our spiritual journey we often feel disoriented, and we may think we have lost our way. Indeed, in starting on the path to salvation, we *have* lost our own way, the ego's way! Realizing that we feel as though we have lost something, and recognizing that because we are feeling loss, we may become afraid, Jesus immediately reassures us: "Think not this is loss." The context of his words, in such cases, is thus the anticipated reaction of our minds to the Course up to that point. That kind of thing happens so often in the Course it is uncanny. Jesus knows us very, very well!

Because this third point clearly addresses the reader's own state of mind, we will return to it for a longer, more detailed discussion in Chapter 17, which is one of the chapters on Application.

Exercise in recognizing when passages address specific situations, issues or beliefs

For this exercise we will *not* use Paragraph 3 from "Choose Once Again." It does indeed speak to a particular kind of situation – namely, trying situations – but it names that type of situation quite explicitly. No detective work is required, therefore. We will instead draw upon other passages in the Course:

> 3. Attack in any form is equally destructive. 4. Its purpose does not change. 5. Its sole intent is murder, and what form of murder serves to cover the massive guilt and frantic fear of punishment the murderer must feel?

6. He may deny he is a murderer and justify his savagery with smiles as he attacks. 7. Yet he will suffer, and will look on his intent in nightmares where the smiles are gone, and where the purpose rises to meet his horrified awareness and pursue him still. 8. For no one thinks of murder and escapes the guilt the thought entails. 9. If the intent is death, what matter the form it takes?

Is death in any form, however lovely and charitable it may seem to be, a blessing and a sign the Voice for God speaks through you to your brother? 2. The wrapping does not make the gift you give. 3. An empty box, however beautiful and gently given, still contains nothing. (T-23.III.1:3-2:3)

1. The specific image in the above passage is that of a murderer who tries to deny that he is a murderer, but who cannot escape the guilt that murder entails, and is haunted in nightmares by what he did. Yet is that what this passage is really about? Try to carry out the guidelines we suggested above.

- Collect the clues. You might, for instance, pay attention to all the references to something covering up an underlying purpose. You might also highlight all of the occurrences of the word "form" or "in any form."
- Identify the overall pattern produced by the clues. There is a form that simultaneously contains and covers up a gift whose purpose is murder.
- Search your mind for a normal situation that fits this pattern. What situation in normal life is this passage talking about?

3. The roads this world can offer seem to be quite large in number, but the time must come when everyone begins to see how like they are to one another. 4. Men have died on seeing this, because they saw no way except the pathways offered by the world. 5. And learning they led nowhere, lost their hope. 6. And yet this was the time they could have learned their greatest lesson. (T-31.IV.3:3-6)

2. If we take this passage literally, it depicts people travelling on different roads in the world, learning these roads do not lead anywhere, and so losing their hope and falling dead. What do you think is the actual situation being talked about here?

> 1. Praise, then, the Father for the perfect sanity of His most holy Son. 2. Your Father knoweth that you have need of nothing. 3. In Heaven this is so, for what could you need in eternity? 4. In your world you do need things. 5. It is a world of scarcity in which you find yourself *because* you are lacking. 6. Yet can you find yourself in such a world? 7. Without the Holy Spirit the answer would be no. 8. Yet because of Him the answer is a joyous *yes!* 9. As Mediator between the two worlds, He knows what you have need of and what will not hurt you. 10. Ownership is a dangerous concept if it is left to you. 11. The ego wants to have things for salvation, for possession is its law. 12. Possession for its own sake is the ego's fundamental creed, a basic cornerstone in the churches it builds to itself. (T-13.VII.10)

3. This paragraph talks on and on about "things" – an

extremely vague word. What exactly are these "things"? Solving this will reveal the specific situation the paragraph is discussing. To solve it, try again to use the guidelines we suggested above. You may be able to solve this rather quickly. If you need more help, read the following pointers:

- Pay attention to all of the words and phrases that suggest something specific. For instance, these things are things we need in this world (Sentence 4). The word "ownership" (Sentence 10) is also a clue, as is the word "possession" (Sentence 12).
- If you assemble these clues, you get: things we need in the world which we can own or possess (and which the ego thinks will bring salvation).
- Does this pattern remind you of anything familiar, anything that would solve the meaning of the word "things"?

ANSWER KEY

1. This passage talks repeatedly about something which is expressed in a "form" (or wrapping) that masks its underlying murderous intent. This something is clearly something we give to others (it is likened to a gift). Finally, this something is overtly identified in the first sentence as "attack." So what the passage is talking about is us attacking in a form that doesn't look like attack. Don't we, like the murderer in the above passage, try to justify our attacks "with smiles," try to make our cruelty to others seem all right by putting on a nice front while we attack? You may want to go back and read the passage again, realizing that the murderer described is really yourself being haunted by guilt over all the attacks you covered over with a smiling facade.

2. The roads are really all the ways of life in the world, all the directions to take in life, all the different ways of finding happiness. As people realize that all of the alternatives in this world get them nowhere, they lose hope and decide to end it all. This passage is talking about *suicide* and how (at least some) people reach that point.

3. These "things," of course, are material possessions. There are other subtle clues about this. First, if you paid close attention to the beginning of this section ten paragraphs earlier, the word "things" was introduced in a line about "stores where people buy an endless list of *things* they do not *need*" (T-13.VII.1:3; italics ours). So, "things" are things you buy in stores. Second, the sentence, "Your Father knoweth that you have need of nothing," is a biblical allusion. The Course never uses an archaic word like "knoweth" unless it is quoting the Bible. In this case, it is quoting the Sermon on the Mount, where Jesus says, "Your heavenly Father knoweth that ye have need of all these things" (Matthew 6:32 KJV), referring to food, drink, and clothing. Once again, "things" refers to material possessions.

Chapter 12

Step II. Interpretation
F. Identifying Irony and Statements of False Arguments

Often the Course will state the ego's arguments in a way meant to reveal how unreasonable and insane they are. It is important to recognize when a statement is intended to be understood as *not true*. The Course does not put these false or ironic statements in quotes or set them off in any way. It would be quite easy to read these lines and think the Course was actually teaching the thoughts they contain.

Example 1:

For instance, I (Allen) once had a question from a study group that asked me to explain a line in Chapter 27 of the Text. "It seems to be saying the exact opposite of things that are said elsewhere in the Course; we don't understand," the writer said. Read by itself, the sentence that was troubling this study group could be confusing; it certainly does seem to contradict things that are said elsewhere in the Course:

> You have no power to make the body stop its evil deeds because you did not make it, and cannot control its actions nor its purpose nor its fate. (T-27.VIII.7:7)

This plainly says that we did *not* make the body. There is no question that this is contradicted elsewhere in the Course. To cite just a few of many instances where we are told we did make the body, and that God did not (emphasis is mine):

> *God did not make the body,* because it is destructible, and therefore not of the Kingdom. (T-6.V.A.2:1)

> From the world of bodies, *made by insanity,* insane messages seem to be returned to *the mind that made it.*
> (T-18.IX.3:1)

> The body is the ego's idol; *the belief in sin made flesh* and then projected outward. (T-20.VI.11:1)

So how can we understand Chapter 27's statement, "you did not make it [the body]"? In a way, understanding this, and recognizing it as a deliberate *false argument,* is an example of the point we covered in Chapter 7: interpreting things by their immediate context. We need to take this sentence in its context. We need to understand the setting in which it occurs.

First of all, the whole section in which the sentence occurs, "The 'Hero' of the Dream," is discussing our dream existence. It opens with the line, "The body is the central figure in the dreaming of the world" (T-27.VIII.1:1). What it is setting out to discuss, quite obviously, is the role the body plays in the ego's dream of worldly, physical existence. The statement, therefore, is occurring in a context which assumes that the body is a *dream figure,* not something real at all.

The paragraph containing this sentence starts by mentioning several ego concepts that are absurd or impossible, such as "a timelessness in which is time made real." Sentences 2 and 3 begin talking about "the world you see" which "depicts exactly what you thought you did. Except that now you think that what you did is being done to you." The remainder of the paragraph then presents *a picture of what we now think*, how we now – from this false perspective – view things.

The final statement about the body, then, is descriptive of how the ego mind sees things, and not how they are in reality. It is the ego that is telling us, "You have no power to make the body stop its evil deeds because you did not make it, and cannot control its actions nor its purpose nor its fate." It is not the author of the Course who is speaking such a message to us! In fact, by putting this statement here, as an expression of the ego's teaching, Jesus is teaching us the exact opposite. He is telling us we *do* have power to make the body stop its "evil" deeds because we *did* make it. We *can* control its actions and its purpose and its fate.

The way we turned the meaning around in the last paragraph is an example of how we can get the most out of such passages. When we recognize that the author is speaking ironically, or deliberately giving voice to a false argument of the ego, we can benefit from reversing what is said, giving voice to the positive message of the author.

Example 2:

For instance, there is another passage, in the Workbook, which makes almost the exact same false argument of the ego:

> To this carefully prepared arena [the world], where angry animals seek for prey and mercy cannot enter, the ego comes to save you. God made you a body. Very well. Let us accept this and be glad. As a body, do not let yourself be deprived of what the body offers. Take the little you can get. God gave you nothing. The body is your only savior. It is the death of God and your salvation. (W-pI.72.6:1–9)

To help ourselves understand what positive truths are implied here, we can reverse what the ego is saying. For example:

> God did not make you a body. Therefore, do not accept this state of affairs; do not accept the body as your identity. Do not think you must avail yourself of what the body offers. Do not settle for the body's meager offerings. God gave you everything. Your body is not your savior; He is. Your body is not your salvation, for it represents the death of God.

Example 3:

Another example of irony or a statement meant to be understood as false is in W-pI.170.6:4. Speaking of false gods, or idols we set up and believe in, the Course says, with tongue in cheek, "It is their enemies who are unreasonable and insane, while they are always merciful and just." The point is, that is how we see ourselves when we are defending our idols. It's always the other guy who seems insane, while we seem to ourselves to be merciful and just, even as we dole out attack and cruelty.

Exercise in identifying irony and statements of false arguments

As in the last chapter, we will have to turn to passages other than the main one we have been using (T-31.VIII.3), because it contains no irony or false arguments.

> 1. Because you think your sins are real, you look on pardon as deception. 2. For it is impossible to think of sin as true and not believe forgiveness is a lie. 3. Thus is forgiveness really but a sin, like all the rest. 4. It says the truth is false, and smiles on the corrupt as if they were as blameless as the grass; as white as snow. 5. It is delusional in what it thinks it can accomplish. 6. It would see as right the plainly wrong; the loathsome as the good.
> (W-pI.134.4:1–6)

1. Read the above passage. What would tell you that the latter part of it is not meant to be read as what the Course is teaching?

2. If Sentences 3-6 do not represent the Course's thinking, whose thinking do they represent?

> 2. Thus do the guilty ones protest their "innocence." 3. Were they not forced into this foul attack by the unscrupulous behavior of the enemy, they would respond with only kindness. 4. But in a savage world the kind cannot survive, so they must take or else be taken from.   (T-23.II.10:2-4)

3. Imagine the last line of the above passage written in calligraphy and framed as a saying from *A Course in Miracles*. How would you show someone why this sentence, though found in the Course, does not represent the teaching of the Course?

> 1. This aspect can grow angry, for the world is wicked and unable to provide the love and shelter innocence deserves. 2. And so this face is often wet with tears at the injustices the world accords to those who would be generous and good. 3. This aspect never makes the first attack. 4. But every day a hundred little things make small assaults upon its innocence, provoking it to irritation, and at last to open insult and abuse. (T-31.V.3)

4. When the above paragraph says, "this aspect" or "this face," it is referring to "the face of innocence," the surface aspect of our self-concept. Whose thought is being expressed in this paragraph? Is it the Course's?

ANSWER KEY

1. The first two sentences say that because you think sin is true you think forgiveness is a lie. The third sentence then begins with "thus," indicating that the statements that follow are based on this kind of thinking.

2. Sentences 3-6 represent our own thinking, based on our belief (mentioned in the first two sentences) that sin is real and forgiveness is a lie.

3. Besides showing them other teachings in the Course that say the opposite, you could take them to this very passage. Based on Sentence 2, we are to understand Sentences 3 and 4 as examples of the apparently guilty ones protesting their innocence, as attackers trying to blame their attacks on something outside themselves.

4. The thought expressed in this paragraph is that of the face of innocence, the surface aspect of our self-concept. This paragraph is both standing outside the face of innocence describing it, and speaking from inside of it, from its standpoint. To capture this double nature of the paragraph, we have inserted various italicized phrases below.

> 1. This aspect can grow angry, for *it believes* the world is wicked and unable to provide the love and shelter innocence deserves. 2. And so this face is often wet with tears at *what it believes are* the injustices the world accords to those who would be generous and good. 3. This aspect *believes that it* never makes the first attack. 4. But every day *it believes* a hundred little things make small assaults upon its innocence, *seemingly* provoking it to irritation, and at last to open insult and abuse. (T-31.V.3)

Chapter 13

Step II. Interpretation
G. Understanding and Appreciating Biblical References

A Course in Miracles quotes and paraphrases the Bible with great frequency. According to Ken Wapnick's *Glossary-Index for "A Course in Miracles,"* the Course contains nearly 900 passages that make direct or indirect reference to the Bible. At this rate, the reader of the Course will come across a biblical reference on the average of almost once per page! This makes understanding and appreciating these references an important aspect of Course interpretation.

These references to Bible verses add a wealth of meaning to the Course passages in which they appear, in at least two ways. First, references to the Bible function in much the same way as the Course's references to itself. When the Course refers to one of its previous discussions, that reference pulls all the meaning of that discussion into the current discussion. This both enriches and clarifies that current discussion.

References to passages in the Bible have the same effect. As an example, in speaking about the body, Chapter 24 of the Text says:

> You brand it sinful and you hate its acts, judging it evil.
> Yet your specialness whispers, "Here is my own beloved son, in whom I am well pleased." (T-24.VII.10:5-6)

This is an obvious allusion to the baptism of Jesus by John the Baptist, where God proclaims, "This is my beloved son, in whom I am well pleased" (Matthew 3:17 KJV). This line is familiar to most. It is part of our fund of Western cultural history and carries the accumulated significance of centuries of Judaeo-Christian religion. In it, God is proclaiming Jesus as His Son, His heir, the apple of His eye, and sending Jesus forth as the one who will carry on His mission in the world.

Understanding all of this adds to the meaning of this passage in the Course. Here, our specialness – our desire to be special – proclaims that our body is its beloved son. Thus, our specialness is cast (most likely by us) in the role of God, and looks upon our body as God looked upon His divine Son, Jesus. Our specialness is sending the body forth in the world on a sacred mission – to serve our god, to make us special.

Recognizing and understanding the biblical allusion in this passage enriches and clarifies it. If you missed the biblical allusion, you would only see that our specialness loves our body like a son. You would not see that our specialness is being cast in the role of God, that our body is being cast in the role of God's divine Son, and that our specialness has sent our body on a sacred mission to do its work in the world, the work of making us special.

The second kind of meaning added by the Course's biblical references is that they often offer a correction for Biblical teachings. This correction is sometimes partial and subtle, sometimes sweeping and fundamental. In either case, the Course is attempting to elevate and purify the concept of God and of salvation that we inherited from Judaeo-Christianity. Even if we were not brought up in a strongly religious family, we have still inherited Judaeo-Christian images of God from our culture. The Course does affirm much of the content of these traditional images, yet it wants to correct much of their content as well. This correction can occur in the briefest of references. For instance, in Chapter 11 we referred to this line from the Text:

> Your Father knoweth that you have need of nothing. In Heaven this is so, for what could you need in eternity? In your world you do need things.   (T-13.VII.10:2-4)

The first sentence contains a subtle reference to Matthew 6:32: "Your heavenly Father knoweth that ye have need of all these things" (KJV) – referring to food, drink, and clothing. Both sentences (in the Course and in the Bible) have almost identical language. Both are talking about material possessions (the Bible verse helps to clarify this fact in the Course, as we mentioned in Chapter 11). Yet they end up saying opposite things. One says that our Father knows that we have need of all kinds of things. The other says that our Father knows that we have need of *nothing*. How can we need nothing? The next line in the Course explains: "In Heaven this is so, for what could you need in eternity?" (T-13.VII.10:3). In our true state in Heaven, we have no needs, for we have everything. We have infinity. And our Father knows that, for He is the One Who gave us infinity.

The Bible verse and the Course passage, then, sketch two different visions of our nature. One implies that we are terrestrial creatures riddled with physical needs, which God will supply. The other implies that we are transcendental spirits who possess all the fullness of Heaven, fullness which God has *eternally* supplied. Here we have a fundamental difference between the biblical outlook and the Course's. Yet we shouldn't press this difference too far, for the Course goes on to say, "In your world you do need things," and explains that the Holy Spirit will supply these material needs if we let Him. It even makes the same point that the Bible does, that having our material needs supplied for us allows us to de-emphasize them and focus on our one true need: the Kingdom of God.

So, in this case, the Course is both agreeing with the Bible's statement about this world – God will provide – and placing that truth atop a different philosophical foundation – God has *already* provided; He has given us an eternal nature which *transcends* this world. The Course is correcting the impression one gets from the Bible that we are separate, needy creatures of this world who may someday be allowed to relocate to Heaven. It is offering a far loftier and more sublime vision of what we really are. And it is providing all of this commentary simply by quoting a single Bible verse and changing the ending from "all these things" to "nothing."

Noticing the biblical allusions in the Course

Of course, before one can receive the benefit of these biblical references, one must first notice them, and this can be quite difficult. In order to notice these references, four things in particular might prove helpful:

First, simply be on the lookout for biblical references. Knowing they are there and keeping your eyes peeled is half the battle.

Second, it helps immensely to know the Bible. The Course was written for a culture steeped in the Bible. The language, thought, and story of the Bible are much of the Course's take-off point. From there, it tries to reshape how we see such biblical concepts as God, sin, miracle, salvation, Heaven, hell, Jesus, etc. But unless you are familiar with its take-off point, much of its reshaping will be lost on you. Simply growing up in a culture with deep biblical roots gives you much of this familiarity. But if you are a serious student of the Course and want to understand it as fully as possible, knowing the Bible first-hand is important. We recommend having read the Bible at least once, and ideally reading it periodically to stay familiar. If you are averse to reading the entire Bible, you can focus on the Gospels, for they are by far the most frequently referred to portion of the Bible. This is to be expected, as they contain the story and teaching of Jesus, the author (or, for those who do not believe this, the purported author) of the Course.

Third, for this purpose it is very helpful to have Ken Wapnick's *Glossary-Index for "A Course in Miracles."* It contains the most complete list available of the Course's biblical references, allowing the reader to look up references from particular sections in the Course or from particular books in the Bible.

Fourth, know the forms in which these references occur. We will review these now:

"The Bible says" or "I said"

Occasionally, the Course openly identifies its biblical references with either "the Bible says" or "I said." Here are some examples:

> Yet the Bible says that a deep sleep fell upon Adam, and nowhere is there reference to his waking up. (T-2.I.3:6)

> This is what the Bible means when it says, "When He shall appear (or be perceived) we shall be like Him, for we shall see Him as He is." (T-3.II.5:10)

> I myself said, "If I go I will send you another Comforter and He will abide with you." (T-5.I.4:4)

Quotation marks

Sometimes the Course will quote a line from the Bible, setting it off with quote marks, but not saying it is from the Bible. For example:

> "God is not mocked" is not a warning but a reassurance. God *would* be mocked if any of His creations lacked holiness. (T-1.V.4:3-4)

Seeing the quotation marks in this passage should let you know the quoted line is from the Bible, simply because the Course does not openly quote from any other work.

King James English

Whenever you come across archaic English in the Course, words like "ye" or "passeth," you can be sure that this is a biblical reference. The Course's own language is contemporary English. However, the Bible translation the Course quotes from is the King James, which is full of "Thee's" and "Thou's." We already saw the passage above which said, "Your Father knoweth that you have need of nothing" (T-13.VII.10:2). The word "knoweth" should tip you off to this being a biblical allusion. Here is another example:

> Thou shalt have no other gods before Him because there *are* none. (T-4.III.6:6)

This, of course, is a reference to the first of the Ten Commandments. Even if you do not know the Ten Commandments, however, the words "thou shalt" lets you know that the Bible is being quoted.

Subtle allusions

Most of the Course's biblical references do not say, "the Bible says," do not have quote marks, and use no King James English. They are simply passing allusions, many of them quite subtle. To identify many, if not most, of these, you will need to be either well-versed in the Bible, or will need to use Ken Wapnick's *Glossary-Index*. For instance, at one point the Course is saying that any encounter with another person is a holy encounter. It then says:

> For I am always there with you, in remembrance of *you*.
> (T-8.III.4:8)

To anyone brought up in church, the latter part of the sentence will sound familiar. It is from the Last Supper, where Jesus institutes the Eucharistic meal of bread and wine and asks his disciples to celebrate this "in remembrance of me" (I Corinthians 11:23-25). This explains why the word "you" is emphasized here in the Course. It is because Jesus is now turning the tables. In the Bible, you are asked to always remember him. Here, he says that he always remembers *you*.

Further, the first part of the above passage is another biblical reference. It refers to Matthew 28:20: "And, lo, I am with you always, even unto the end of the world."

How to interpret the biblical references

Once you identify a reference to the Bible, you then have to interpret it. We recommend a four-step process in doing this:

1. Locate the reference in the Bible and read the Bible passage.

When you think the Course is referring to the Bible, look up and read the Bible passage referred to. We use either a Bible concordance (preferably for the King James Version) or Ken Wapnick's *Glossary-Index*.

2. Try to understand what the Bible passage is saying.

While reading the Bible passage, try to get a sense for what it is about, what its main thrust is. Having some understanding of it is crucial for the remaining two steps. Here again, familiarity with the Bible is a great aid in understanding the Course.

3. See what light the Bible passage throws on the Course passage.

We said above that understanding the biblical allusion can

add meaning and clarity to the Course passage. So, once you have read and understood the Bible passage, read the Course passage in light of it. Try to see what dimensions it adds to the Course passage. See if it clarifies anything that was fuzzy about the Course passage.

4. See what commentary the Course passage makes about the Bible passage.

As we said above, the Course passages very often make indirect commentary on the Bible verses they allude to. To understand this commentary, note any ways in which the Course reference differs from the Bible verse it refers to. This difference is the root of the commentary, so look at it, think about it, try to understand its implications.

Example

Let's use an example that we already cited above:

> "God is not mocked" is not a warning but a reassurance. God *would* be mocked if any of His creations lacked holiness. (T-1.V.4:3-4)

First, find the Bible passage and read it. You might look up the word "mocked" in a Bible concordance. Or you might use Wapnick's *Glossary-Index*. Either one will let you know that this is a reference to Galatians:

> God is not mocked: for whatsoever a man soweth, that shall he also reap. (Gal 6:7)

Second, try to understand this Bible verse. It means that God cannot truly be defied (to defy is one of the meanings of "mock"). When you break His laws, you will not escape His punishment. God remains the sovereign power. Even when you go against His power, it has the final word.

Third, see what light the Bible verse throws on the Course passage. As we just noted, the Bible verse says that God remains the sovereign power. His power always has the final say. When we insert that meaning into the Course passage, we do find clarification. Now we understand why "God would be mocked if any of His creations lacked holiness." If God created you pure and holy, then to defile your holiness would be a mockery of God. It would mean that His power is not the last word, but can be overruled by another power. But because He is the sovereign power, even when you try to defile your nature with sin, you cannot do it. God's power is all-determining. God is not mocked.

Fourth, see what commentary the Course passage is making on the Bible verse, by taking note of any differences between the two. The Course here is offering a deep correction to the biblical passage. It says the fact that God is not mocked "is not a warning." This is a big difference, for in the Bible, "God is not mocked" *is* a warning. It says, "Do good or God will punish you." The Course is refuting that. According to it, "God is not mocked" is really "a reassurance." How so? The next sentence provides the answer. It is reassuring to know that, no matter what you do, you can never defile the holiness God gave you when He created you. Thus, from the same starting place, the Bible and the Course derive opposite conclusions. One says that when you sin you will not escape your punishment, for God is not mocked. The other says that you *cannot* sin, for God is not mocked. Here, then, the Course is offering us a new concept of God's sovereign power. That God is the ultimate power, the final word, is not a guarantee of our punishment, but a guarantee of our *innocence.*

Thus, when we truly understand and appreciate this biblical reference, we find essential clarification for the Course passage in which it is found, as well as profound correction for biblical teaching.

Exercise in understanding and appreciating biblical references

Here we will use a single sentence from Paragraph 3 of "Choose Once Again":

> He would not leave you comfortless, alone in dreams of hell, but would release your mind from everything that hides His face from you. (T-31.VIII.3:5)

1. Do you notice anything that sounds like a biblical reference here? If not, consult Ken Wapnick's *Glossary-Index,* if you have one. If not, just look in the answer key.

2. What does it mean to not leave someone comfortless? You might want to look up the word "comfort" in the dictionary. You may also want to look up the word "desolate," which is the word that the Revised Standard Version of the Bible uses instead of "comfortless."

3. What did "I will not leave you comfortless; I will come to you" mean in its original context in the Bible? You may want to look at the verse that follows it: "Yet a little while, and the world will see me no more, but you will see me; because I live, you will live also" (RSV).

Bringing the Course to Life

4. Now look at the whole of Sentence 5. Can you find any other references to the idea of Christ not leaving you alone?

5. In light of this Biblical verse, do you see a new thrust to the sentence? Try to write a summary of the sentence that captures its main thrust as you now see it.

6. Do you notice any differences between the biblical passage and the Course passage? Do you see any possible commentary on the biblical passage contained in these differences?

7. There is another possible biblical allusion in Sentence 5 above (Robert's wife, Susan spotted this, demonstrating that it *is* possible to notice these references even if one is not a Bible scholar). "Everything that hides His face from you" sounds like an allusion to the biblical theme of God hiding His face from us. This theme is found especially frequently in the Psalms, where the author often beseeches God to not hide His face. Here are some examples:

> How long, O Lord? Wilt thou forget me for ever? How long wilt thou hide thy face from me?   (Ps 13:1)

> Why dost thou hide thy face? Why dost thou forget our affliction and oppression?   (Ps 44:24)

> Hide not thy face from thy servant; for I am in distress, make haste to answer me.   (Ps 69:17)

Based on these verses, what did it mean for God to hide His face from us in the Bible?

8. Now compare the meaning of the hidden face of the Divine in the biblical passages and in the Course passage above. How do the two meanings differ?

9. What commentary is the Course offering on the biblical idea via these differences?

ANSWER KEY

1. "He would not leave you comfortless" is a reference to John 14:18: "I will not leave you comfortless: I will come to you" (KJV).

2. "I will not leave you comfortless" simply means, "I will not leave you in the pain of aloneness." Thus, the following phrase in the Bible verse: "I will come to you." Comfortless is defined as being without assistance, support, or solace. Webster's defines "desolate" as: "joyless, disconsolate and sorrowful through or as if through separation from a loved one." The New King James Version of the Bible uses the phrase "I will not leave you orphans." All of this reinforces the idea that comfortless refers to the experience of being alone, abandoned.

3. Originally, this verse was a statement that, even though Jesus was going to leave the disciples – he was going to be killed – he would still be present with them in spirit. His presence would be within them.

4. The word "alone" is an obvious reference to aloneness. "Hell" is also a subtle reference to aloneness; hell is often understood as a state of total separation from God. Releasing you "from everything that hides His face from you" is also a reference to not leaving you alone, for this process leaves you face-to-face with Christ. So in this sentence we now see four references to the idea of aloneness: "comfortless," "alone," "hell," and a condition in which His face is hidden from you.

5. The sentence's main thrust is not that Christ would release you from hell. It is far more specific than that. It is that Christ would rescue you from the hell of aloneness and lift you into a face-to-face encounter with Him. *He would substitute the pain of your aloneness with the joy of His presence.* Both of these latter sentences could be used as summaries of Sentence 5.

6. The main difference between the biblical passage and the Course passage is this: One is about Jesus not leaving his disciples comfortless when he physically leaves them; the other is about Christ, our true Self, not leaving us comfortless by helping us make a better choice us in all situations. This seems to reflect the Course's greater stress on what we might call a historical truths, truths that are not dependent on particular events in history. The individual known as Jesus leaving his disciples but remaining with them in spirit – these are historical truths. The universal Self in everyone helping all individuals choose better in all situations – these are *ahistorical* truths. Even though the Course does emphasize some historical truths (particularly, the saving power of the life of Jesus), as we see here, its main emphasis is on a historical truths.

7. Based on these passages, for God to hide His face seems to have meant for Him to turn His attention and help away from you. It meant that He didn't answer your prayers and relieve your affliction.

8. In the Bible, God is the One doing the hiding. Further, turning His face toward you seems to have the purpose of helping you with your external affairs. In the Course, the face of Christ is hidden from you by your own false images. The

Divine is not hiding from you; He wants to remove all that would keep you from seeing His face. Further, seeing His face seems to have the purpose of receiving *inner* (rather than outer) help, comfort, and solace.

9. The Course here seems to be subtly correcting the Bible by saying that the Divine is not hiding His face from us; we are covering our eyes. He wants to reveal His face to us. He wants to gently and lovingly pry our hands from our eyes. The delay in seeing His face, therefore, comes from us, not Him. (This same point is implied by another allusion to one of these same biblical verses. The first Psalm we quoted above asks, "How long, O Lord?" The Course turns this around and asks, "How long, O Son of God?" [W-pII.4.5:1])

The Course also seems to be correcting the Bible by implying that the purpose of seeing the face of the Divine is not to receive outer help, but inner enlightenment. The purpose of seeing the face of the Divine is to discover Who we really are.

Chapter 14

Step II. Interpretation
H. Summarizing the Message

The final interpretation technique is very simple to express: Summarize the message. Summarizing is always helpful in deepening our understanding. Sometimes it can result in a major "Aha!" experience. If you have time for it, it is always worthwhile.

We suggest four methods we have found useful in trying to summarize a portion of the Text, usually a section. (It isn't out of the question to try to summarize a whole chapter, but as you might guess, it isn't easy.)

1. Assemble the structure

Often, while reading a particular section in the Course, you can sense that several ideas are being combined into a larger structure of thought. Understanding how the various ideas fit together into such a structure can immensely clarify what you are reading. It can provide you with an "aerial view" of a section or a significant part of that section.

Example

> 1. The escape from darkness involves two stages: First, the recognition that darkness cannot hide. 2. This step usually entails fear. 3. Second, the recognition that there is nothing you want to hide even if you could. 4. This step brings escape from fear. 5. When you have become willing to hide nothing, you will not only be willing to enter into communion but will also understand peace and joy.
>
> 1. Holiness can never be really hidden in darkness, but you can deceive yourself about it. 2. This deception makes you fearful because you realize in your heart it *is* a deception, and you exert enormous efforts to establish its reality. (T-1.IV.1:1-2:2)

In this passage you may be able to sense that a conceptual structure is being assembled. The first thing that might alert you to this is that two things are talked about as being hidden: both darkness (1:1) and holiness (2:1). After you notice that, you can look around for more pieces of the puzzle. You can see that neither darkness nor holiness can actually be hidden (1:2, 2:1). Then you might see that, in both cases, the realization that you cannot really hide them brings fear, fear that they will come out into the light.

The question then becomes: How does our attempt to hide our darkness relate to our attempt to hide our holiness? If these two ideas are part of a larger structure of ideas, how do they relate to each other? Where does each one fit in that larger structure?

This passage implies that when you bring darkness up into

the light, you escape from it (1:1). It is gone. And this brings you back in touch with peace, joy (see 1:5), and presumably, holiness. Based on this (and on the rest of the Course's teaching), the structure implied here probably looks like this:

- The top layer is your awareness. Darkness and holiness here are not physically hidden, but hidden from your awareness. The very idea of "hidden" here thus implies two levels: what you are aware of and what is hidden from your awareness.
- Right below your awareness is your darkness.
- Below your darkness is your holiness. It is hidden by your darkness, covered by it. We know this because, when the darkness is gone, your holiness comes back into your awareness.

Teasing out such a structure is usually not easy. It takes a lot of detective work, as well as checking your work against what the Course has said and then refining your conclusions. However, if you feel drawn to this kind of thing, one suggestion is to draw small diagrams in the white space on the pages of your Course. Get a very fine-pointed pen and draw the structure that is forming in your mind's eye as you read. You might use boxes to identify the various parts of the structure, and then, using lines and arrows, label how those boxes relate to each other. For instance, the above structure of three levels (your awareness, your darkness, your holiness) could easily be diagrammed in such a way.

2. Locate key sentences

Locate the key sentence or sentences in a paragraph. That means, try to find a single sentence in each paragraph that seems to state the main thought of the paragraph. You may not always find a single sentence that does this. Sometimes you might find it necessary to pick two sentences. If you are comfortable with marking your book, you may want to underline or highlight the key sentences you pick in some way that identifies them, perhaps putting a "K" in the margin.

Example 1:

The key sentence of T-31.VIII.5 might be, "Learn the happy habit of response to all temptation."

You may wish to try finding the key sentence or sentences for an entire section. Occasionally there is one sentence that expresses an entire section's message; sometimes, stringing three or four sentences from the section together will provide a nice summary.

Example 2:

The latter half of T-14.III, "The Decision for Guiltlessness," beginning with Paragraph 11, is very well summed up by the following key sentences taken mostly from the first line of several paragraphs:

- It will never happen that you must make decisions for yourself.
- The One Who knows the plan of God that God would have you follow can teach you what it is.
- Let Him, therefore, be the only Guide that you would follow to salvation.
- Say to the Holy Spirit only, "Decide for me," and it is done.
- Unlearn isolation through His loving guidance, and learn of all the happy communication that you have thrown away but could not lose.

Example 3:

We also like this "key sentence summary" of the last half of T-13.VII, "Attainment of the Real World":

- Everything the ego tells you that you need will hurt you.
- Only the Holy Spirit knows what you need.
- Leave, then, your needs to Him.
- ...remember what you really want...
- Then follow Him in joy.

3. One-sentence summaries of paragraphs

Another useful method is trying to write, in your own words, a single sentence that sums up the main thought of each paragraph. Most paragraphs have one primary thought they are trying to express, with all the sentences contributing different parts to that main thought. Some paragraphs, especially very long ones, may have more than one main thought, in which case you will need to use two summary sentences.

To summarize an entire paragraph in one or two sentences, here are some helpful questions you can ask yourself:

1) What are the main themes, and how do they relate to each other?
2) What problem is being described?
3) What results does it produce?
4) What is the solution given (and its results)?

Using T-31.VIII.5 again as an example, we might summarize the paragraph as follows:

> Respond to any temptation to see yourself as weak with the choice for holiness, "I am as God created me," because repeating these words removes the illusion of alternative choices and makes miracles natural.

4. Summarizing an entire section

The final summary method is writing a short paragraph that summarizes the main message of an entire section. A summary cannot possibly include every detail of a section and be a summary; you must be selective about what you include. If there is a main theme and several sub-themes, a good summary may need to leave out all or most of the sub-themes.

I (Allen) usually do section summaries after I have spent a lot of time studying every individual paragraph. By that time, I have a fairly good feel for where the section is trying to go, and what it is trying to get across; that "good feel" becomes the seed for my summary. Before I try to write the summary, I will read the entire section over quickly, perhaps two or three times, trying to get the overall sense of it. And then, I write. As an example, here is a section summary for the last section of the Text, "Choose Once Again" (T-31.VIII):

> Every situation in our lives is offering us another chance to choose between the temptation to see ourselves and our brothers as weak and miserable bodies, and seeing the strength of Christ in us. How we choose to see our brothers determines how we see our own identity; in giving the gift of seeing with Christ to others we find the Christ in ourselves, and in so doing become saviors to the world. We will accept this gift, join Jesus as saviors, and the song of thanks will fill the world.

I (Robert) used to engage in a detailed process of summarizing each section. I would first summarize each paragraph in the section. Then I would write a summary of the major themes of that section, usually describing between four and six major themes. Then I would teach the section to a group.

After these three steps I would finally write a brief summary (about three lines) of that section. Quite often, the whole section would come together in my mind only after these three steps; only then did it resolve itself into a unity for me. Here are some of my summaries for sections in Chapter 20 of the Text:

II. The Gift of Lilies

If the body is your chosen home you will give your savior its gifts, which are thorns. But you joined with him and so accepted the vision that sees only lilies. Give these to him and his holiness will lead you to your new chosen home, Heaven.

III. Sin as an Adjustment

The ego adjusts truth to fit its orders, making a world that mirrors self-condemnation. Do not ask it what truth is. Ask the Holy Spirit, and you will see a world reflecting your innocence, and realize that your relationship is healed and you are free.

IV. Entering the Ark

Give power to sin and it will imprison you. See the power of sinlessness in your brother and he will free you. Concentrate only on your part in the Holy Spirit's plan and He will take care of the rest.

You may notice that these summaries seem to follow a similar pattern. It is a pattern that can be used to summarize many of the Text sections. The pattern might be expressed in this way:

You have chosen the ego.
These have been the results.

Instead of choosing the ego, now choose God.
And these will be the results.

Exercise in summarizing the message

In this exercise we will summarize the message of Paragraph 3 from "Choose Once Again." To help us in doing this, let's first review the things we have learned about this paragraph in our earlier chapters:

Chapter 7

- In your trials, Christ is trying to teach you the opposite kind of lesson from the lesson temptation would teach you.
- You may think your body's power is the only strength you have, but Christ's power is your real strength.
- You have chosen to remain in hell, but Christ would not leave you there.
- Each time you choose, you are choosing between learning the lesson and your past failure to learn the lesson, between remaining in hell versus helping everyone out of hell, between your weakness and the strength of Christ in you.
- The reference to Christ calling you (Sentence 2) is a reference to an earlier description of Christ appearing to you in all His glory asking you to choose once again.

Chapter 8

- "Trials" are the same as difficulties, distresses and perplexities.
- Christ is what "He" and "His" refer to throughout most of the paragraph.
- Christ is defined as the Self that God created you as.
- The "source of pain" (Sentence 3) is your choice to not learn the lesson. Thus, Christ would remove your choice to

not learn the lesson, and thereby remove your pain.
- "Hell" is not an afterlife condition, but your current condition of perceiving a terrifying world. Thus, Christ wants to deliver you from your current hellish condition.
- The images that veil the truth (Sentence 3) are false images of yourself. These are also what hide Christ's face from you (Sentence 5). Thus, Christ would deliver you from your false self-images.

Chapter 9
- Here are some attempts to reduce Sentence 1 to its basic essence:
    - Trials are unlearned lessons presented again so that now you can learn them.
    - Trials are lessons you chose to not learn presented again so that now you can make a different choice.
    - A trial is an opportunity to choose again and escape the pain a previous poor choice brought to you.
- Here is an attempt to reduce Sentence 2 to its gist:

    In every trial Christ asks you to choose again.

Chapter 10
- Here is the logic contained in Sentence 4:

    Christ would remove everything that does not reflect the condition in which God created you.

    God created you joyous.

    Therefore, Christ would remove everything from you that is not joyous.

- Here is the logic contained in Sentence 6:

    Christ is the only Power that is really in you.

Christ is holy.
Christ's holiness is in you; His holiness is yours.

- Here is the logic contained in Sentence 7:

   Christ is the Self that God created as His Son.
   You are God's Son.
   Christ is your Self.

   Christ is your Self. All He has is yours.
   Christ is strong.
   Christ's strength is yours.

Chapter 13

- Sentence 5 contains a biblical reference that helps reveal what the sentence really means, which is this:

   Christ would rescue you from the hell of aloneness by coming to you and lifting you into a face-to-face encounter with Him. He would substitute the pain of your loneliness with the joy of His presence.

With the above discoveries to fill out your understanding, read through the paragraph once again:

   1. Trials are but lessons that you failed to learn presented once again, so where you made a faulty choice before you now can make a better one, and thus escape all pain that what you chose before has brought to you. 2. In every difficulty, all distress, and each perplexity Christ calls to you and gently says, "My brother, choose again." 3. He would not leave one source of pain unhealed, nor any image left to veil the truth. 4. He would remove all misery from you whom God created altar unto joy. 5. He would not leave you comfortless, alone in dreams of hell, but would release your mind

from everything that hides His face from you. 6. His holiness is yours because He is the only Power that is real in you. 7. His strength is yours because He is the Self That God created as His only Son.   (T-31.VIII.3)

1. Pick a key sentence, the one which in your mind best summarizes the paragraph.

2. This paragraph has a definite structure. It can be seen to proceed in three phases:

Phase 1. Sentences 1 and 2

Phase 2. Sentences 3, 4, and 5 (Notice the parallel language: "He would not leave...He would remove"; "He would not leave...but would release.")

Phase 3. Sentences 6 and 7 (Notice the parallel language: "His____is yours because He is the...")

Try to capture the essence of Phase 1 – the idea that its sentences have in common. Then do the same with Phase 2 and Phase 3. Write these down, if you will, and then refer to the Answer Key before going on.

3. Now, at long last, we are in a position to see what this paragraph is really saying. To see the overall picture of the paragraph, you need to connect the three phases. Now, then, try to find themes or persons that run through all three phases.

4. Now see if you can track the theme of "Christ and you" as it proceeds through all three phases. This really provides the key to understanding the paragraph as a whole. Phase 1 describes what Christ does. Phases 2 and 3 describe *why* He does this, what result He is trying to achieve. If you want to try writing this out (and we genuinely encourage you to do so) you might use this form: "Christ does this in relation to me (Phase 1). He does it for this reason, to achieve this result

(Phase 2). And ultimately for this reason, to achieve this final result (Phase 3)."

5. Based on how the three phases of this paragraph tie together, try writing a one- or two-sentence summary of the paragraph.

ANSWER KEY

1. This is very subjective. There is no single right answer. We picked Sentence 2: "In every difficulty, all distress, and each perplexity Christ calls to you and gently says, 'My brother, choose again.'"

2. Phase 1: Every trying situation is a call from Christ to choose differently than you did in the past.
Phase 2: Christ would not leave you in the pain of your past choices but would release you from their pain.
Phase 3: Everything that Christ has is yours because He is your Self.

3. Christ and you. Each phase contains some kind of interaction or relation between Christ and you.

4. Seeing the paragraph as a whole really depends on seeing the link between Phase 2 and 3. This is very difficult, for much is implied, not stated. To see the link, we can put an additional sentence in between Sentences 5 and 6:

> He would not leave you...alone in dreams of hell, but would release your mind from everything that hides His face from you. When this has been accomplished, when literally nothing stands between you and Him, what else would you realize but this: His holiness is yours because He is the only Power that is real in you.

In light of the above, here is our attempt to capture the theme of Christ and you as it moves from Phase 1 to 2 to 3:

> Christ calls to me in the midst of all my trials, asking me to make a different choice. He does this because He would not leave me stuck in the pain of my past choices, but would release me. He would come to me and lift me out of the lonely hell I made (via my past choices) so that I can see His face and feel His presence. Seeing His face I will realize that all He has is mine because He is my Self.

The paragraph, in other words, says that Christ presents me with lessons in my life and then explains why: so that I can be released from my self-made hell, come face-to-face with Him and realize that He is my Self. Christ first appears to me as a lesson-giver so that He can then become my companion and finally reveal Himself to me as my Self. The paragraph, then, links together the more terrestrial idea of learning lessons in concrete situations with the more lofty idea of realizing my true Self. It links them together by saying that the One Who presents me with the lessons *is* my true Self, and that He does so as a way of revealing Himself *as* my Self.

5. Here is a one-sentence summary of this paragraph:

> Christ presents me with lessons in all my trials so that I may leave the lonely hell I made, come face-to-face with Him, and realize that He is my Self.

* * * * * *

We have done an incredible amount of work on a single paragraph – in both this chapter and previous chapters – but not because we expect Course students to delve into each paragraph in this kind of exhaustive detail. We ourselves do not usually delve into paragraphs this completely. We are only doing so here for the sake of this book!

As we said in the Introduction, the reason we have mined this paragraph so thoroughly is simply to show how much meaning is there waiting for you in each and every paragraph. We want to demonstrate that your efforts at study will be rewarded with greater comprehension and appreciation. So please don't be daunted by the amount of work we have put into this paragraph (and we aren't done yet). We are not expecting you to be this thorough. We simply want to give you a glimpse of the possibilities.

Chapter 15

Step III. Application
A. Experiencing and Visualizing the Passage

Beginning with this chapter, we will now cover the Application techniques.

III. Application: What does it mean to me?

First of all, what do we mean by "application"? This is how we summarized it in Chapter 4:

Here, in the third step, you bring the words of the Course into direct contact with your life. You attempt to experience, or perhaps visualize, what the passage is talking about; many images in the Course lend themselves to this practice. You read it as personally addressing you, perhaps changing "you" statements into "I" statements. You attempt to carry out specific instructions that might be given. You dialogue with the author, asking him questions or turning what you read into a prayer. You relate the principles given to specific areas in your life: your needs, problems and concerns.

A. Experience and visualize the passage

The first type of application is visualizing or experiencing a passage in your mind. To experience a passage means to let the ideas sink in deeply enough to evoke an emotional response in you. You let your mind focus on the passage and dwell on all that it implies for you. For instance, take the words from the Introduction to the Text: "Nothing real can be threatened." Try to imagine all that means if it is really true. How would you live your life if that were true, and you fully believed it?

When I (Allen) think about those words, and what they mean to me if they are really true and I really believe them, I start feeling very safe. I begin to realize that I cannot – ever – possibly be in any real danger. Real things cannot be threatened; only illusions can be threatened, and they are not real. So I cannot possibly suffer the loss of anything that is real. Any loss that I do seem to experience must be either an illusion of loss, or the loss of an illusion. Any danger that I think I am facing is either the illusion of a threat, or only the threat of an illusion. I can't lose! I can't be hurt. As the Course very plainly teaches in several places, I am invulnerable (for instance, see T-1.IV.2:11; T-4.VII.8:3; T-13.I.8:1; T-14.III.10:1; T-31.VI.6).

As I let those words and their meaning sink in, I begin to feel very calm and peaceful. I begin to feel the grasping, protective, defensive attitude of my mind relaxing and softening. I can sink back into the arms of God. I can open my heart safely.

How does what is said make you feel? How would you feel if you really believed it? Those are the questions you must ask yourself to experience a passage. Ideally, you will go beyond simply thinking, "If I believed this I would feel peaceful," to actually feeling peaceful.

To visualize a passage means taking images from the passage, closing your eyes if that helps, and trying to imagine them visually. Try to picture the scene that is being described, supplying the details, the color, the sounds and smells. When it speaks of the lawns of Heaven, picture the great, green expanse of it. Imagine that you can smell the fresh grass. Bring the passage to life for yourself.

Example 1:

> You *are* as God created you, and so is every living thing you look upon, regardless of the images you see. What you behold as sickness and as pain, as weakness and as suffering and loss, is but temptation to perceive yourself defenseless and in hell. Yield not to this, and you will see all pain, in every form, wherever it occurs, but disappear as mists before the sun. (T-31.VIII.6:1–3)

Read this over several times to get all the parts of it in your mind. Then, close your eyes. Picture someone you know, someone you have looked upon recently in whom you have seen sickness and pain, or weakness, or suffering, or loss. It should not be too difficult to find a subject to work with. Realize that the pain or loss you see in this other person is somehow a projection of your mind's desire to see *yourself* as defenseless and in hell. In other words, you are seeing this other person as defenseless and in hell because, unconsciously, that is how you want to see yourself.

Consciously choose *not* to see yourself that way. Perhaps you may affirm, "I do not want to see myself defenseless or in hell, nor do I want to see my sister that way." Try to visualize yourself affirming this and meaning it, and then visualize the pain or sickness or weakness you have been seeing simply disappearing as mists before the sun. Picture a morning mist; imagine the way it just dwindles into nothing as the sun brightens. Say to yourself, "As this mist disappears in the sunlight, so my brother's pain is disappearing in the light of Christ. I am as God created me, and so is he." Imagine the mists of pain and loss disappearing, revealing the loveliness of Christ they were hiding.

Example 2:

Some of the imagery in the Course practically begs the readers to immerse themselves in the picture being presented. For instance:

> The special relationship has the most imposing and deceptive frame of all the defenses the ego uses. Its thought system is offered here, surrounded by a frame so heavy and so elaborate that the picture is almost obliterated by its imposing structure. Into the frame are woven all sorts of fanciful and fragmented illusions of love, set with dreams of sacrifice and self-aggrandizement, and interlaced with gilded threads of self-destruction. The glitter of blood shines like rubies, and the tears are faceted like diamonds and gleam in the dim light in which the offering is made.
>
> Look at the *picture.* Do not let the frame distract you. This gift is given you for your damnation, and if you take it you will believe that you *are* damned. You cannot have the frame without the picture. What you value is the frame, for there you see no conflict. Yet the frame is

only the wrapping for the gift of conflict. The frame is not the gift. Be not deceived by the most superficial aspects of this thought system, for these aspects enclose the whole, complete in every aspect. Death lies in this glittering gift. Let not your gaze dwell on the hypnotic gleaming of the frame. Look at the picture, and realize that death is offered you. (T-17.IV.8:1–9:11)

Here you have the Course giving you very specific instructions: "Look at the *picture*." Can't you just see this picture and frame in your mind's eye – a grotesque photo of Death itself, surrounded by a glittering frame of rubies and diamonds that *seem* so lovely that you almost want to let your attention stay on the frame and ignore the awful picture it surrounds. Can't you imagine someone, Jesus perhaps, shaking your arm and saying, "Look at the picture, friend! Look at the picture, not the frame!" Isn't it true that sometimes the fantasies surrounding our special relationships have blinded us to their reality, just like this?

We think you can see that this kind of practice – visualizing and experiencing the passages you read – can make the Course very practical to you. You will find as well that focusing on it in this way greatly increases your understanding of what is being said. The greater understanding, in turn, enriches your practical application.

Noticing and putting together a visual image

Many of the Course's images, like the example above, are readily identifiable. Many others are quite subtle. They are not only difficult to notice, but also difficult to put together. Yet, obviously, before you can visualize an image, you must know that an image is there and what the image is. This application step, therefore, has both an observation step and an interpretation step that precede it. We did cover the observation step in Chapter 5. However, we did not explicitly cover the interpretation technique. Let us, therefore, summarize here the entire procedure (Observation, Interpretation, and Application) that you would go through in relation to a visual image in the Course:

1. Simply *observe* that the author has painted a visual picture. Watch for this, looking especially for visual words like "face," "door," "thorns," etc.

2. Put the image together. Sometimes the image will be immediately clear. Yet at other times you will need to read very carefully in order to mentally assemble the image as a whole. Just collect all the clues you have, all the visual-sounding words and phrases in a particular passage. Then try to fit them together, like puzzle pieces, into a whole picture.

3. Try to understand the meaning of the image. The image is a symbol. It symbolizes some idea the Course is teaching in that passage. The whole purpose of the image is to make that idea more vivid, alive and impactful. So it is important to understand what that idea is, what the image symbolizes.

4. Actually visualize the image while being aware of its meaning. Try to picture it in your mind's eye while holding in mind what it means. This gives you the full benefit of the image.

Example 1:

> The closer you come to the foundation of the ego's thought system, the darker and more obscure becomes

the way. Yet even the little spark in your mind is enough to lighten it. Bring this light fearlessly with you, and bravely hold it up to the foundation of the ego's thought system. Be willing to judge it with perfect honesty. Open the dark cornerstone of terror on which it rests, and bring it out into the light. There you will see that it rested on meaninglessness, and that everything of which you have been afraid was based on nothing.

My brother, you are part of God and part of me. When you have at last looked at the ego's foundation without shrinking you will also have looked upon ours. I come to you from our Father to offer you everything again. Do not refuse it in order to keep a dark cornerstone hidden, for its protection will not save you. I give you the lamp and I will go with you. You will not take this journey alone. I will lead you to your true Father, Who hath need of you, as I have. Will you not answer the call of love with joy? (T-11.IN.3:5-4:8)

Now let's go through our four steps. First, you can tell there is an image here. How? By the presence of visual words and phrases such as "spark," "bravely hold it up," "dark cornerstone," and "lamp."

Second, let's assemble the image. Let's first collect the clues. You are coming closer and closer to the ego's foundation. You are bringing with you a light (it sounds like you are walking and carrying some kind of lamp). When you reach the ego's foundation, you hold your light up to it. The ego's foundation is then described as a dark cornerstone, which you open (a reference to the practice of placing things like time capsules inside of cornerstones). The second paragraph then adds Jesus into this image, saying that he will give you the lamp and go with you on this journey.

Apparently, you are walking with Jesus through a dark corridor under a building (since a cornerstone is part of the foundation of a building). You reach the cornerstone, hold your light up to that cornerstone, open it up, and realize it contains nothing. Then you are able to see your true foundation.

Third, what does this image symbolize? This is not too difficult. It symbolizes a journey into the hidden foundation of your ego, a journey into the depths of your psyche.

Fourth, let's visualize this image holding its meaning in mind. With a little embellishment, we might picture it in this way:

> We see ourselves on an expedition into the hidden chambers of our ego. In this journey we find ourselves underground beneath some massive building, the edifice of the ego. We might see ourselves walking down a dark, dank corridor, approaching some nameless horror, the way getting ever "darker and more obscure." Yet Jesus is with us, leading us along the path, handing us a lamp – the light of truth – to light our way. We feel our hand in his. At last we see it looming up ahead, "the dark cornerstone of terror" on which the ego's entire edifice is built. With Jesus beside us, we bravely hold the light of reason up to this dark cornerstone. We then open it up, and calmly see, once and for all, that it contains nothing – no great hidden secrets, stored there for centuries – *nothing*. We see with our own eyes that the ego's foundation is completely hollow, vacuous. This

allows us to look past its empty foundation to our true foundation in God. We might imagine looking past the dark cornerstone and seeing an opening, a window onto Heaven.

Example 2:

> And yet, your mind holds only what you think with God. Your self-deceptions cannot take the place of truth [what you think with God]. No more than can a child who throws a stick into the ocean change the coming and the going of the tides, the warming of the water by the sun, the silver of the moon on it by night.
>
> (W-pI.rIV.IN.4:1-3)

This wonderful image is readily identifiable. It requires no detective work. So the first two steps are done without thinking. But what does it mean? It symbolizes the idea (which we are being instructed to practice for ten days), "My mind holds only what I think with God." This means that when God created my mind, He placed in it my real thoughts. These real thoughts are stable, formless and infinite realities that God and I think together in perfect unison. These are all my mind really holds. Yet I think I have replaced these eternal thoughts with my little thoughts about breakfast, the weather and the duties of the day. I think these have actually changed the character of my mind.

Let us visualize the image while remembering what it symbolizes. You are the child. As you visualize yourself on the beach, throwing a stick into the ocean, you realize this is you throwing a thought into your mind. You believe this thought actually remolds your mind, banishing whatever grand thoughts that God placed there in the beginning. Yet your mind is not some little pool that you established. It is an ocean whose grandeur was established by God. And so you see your stick simply floating on the unchanged ocean. As it floats, you see the water being slowly warmed as the sun's rays shine upon it. After the sun goes down you see the water calmly reflecting the light of the moon. And while the wheel of the days and nights continues to turn, you see the tides come and go as they always have. You see the ocean's stately rhythms proceed exactly as they have from time immemorial, unheeding of your little stick. And as you do, you realize your true mind continues in just this same way, unaffected by your little thoughts.

Exercise in experiencing and visualizing the passage

For this exercise, we will again turn to the passage we have used for most of the exercises (T-31.VIII.3), and we will also use an additional passage from elsewhere in the Course.

1. Read Paragraph 3 of "Choose Once Again" (printed below) and try to experience it in the way we discussed earlier. As you read each sentence, imagine that the sentence really is true and applies to you right now. See how you feel as a result. We will provide a few additional comments to aid this process.

> 1. Trials [in your life] are but lessons that you failed to learn presented once again [so that's why those trying situations keep happening], so where you made a faulty choice before you now can make a better one, and thus escape all pain that what you chose before

has brought to you [imagine that you really can escape the pain you caused yourself, just by making a better choice].

2. In every difficulty, all distress, and each perplexity [in your life] Christ calls to you [personally] and gently says, "My brother [insert your name], choose again."

3. He would not leave one source of pain unhealed [He cares about you that much], nor any image left to veil the truth [imagine all your false-images being removed, leaving you face-to-face with the truth].

4. He would remove all misery from you whom God created altar unto joy [How would it feel to have all your misery removed from you?].

5. He would not leave you comfortless, alone in dreams of hell [He really doesn't want you left alone], but would release your mind from everything that hides His face from you [He wants you to see His face; imagine what seeing His face would feel like].

6. His holiness is yours because He is the only Power that is real in you [entertain, for a moment, the possibility that Christ's holiness really is yours].

7. His strength is yours [what would it feel like to know that you possess the strength of Christ?] because He is the Self That God created as His only Son [imagine that you really are God's beloved Son].

2. Sentence 2 is not exactly a visual image (though its counterpart in Paragraph 1:4-5 is), but it does have an auditory component. You can therefore imagine *hearing* it. So do that. Imagine being in a trying situation and audibly hearing

Christ, the true Self in all beings, call to you and say, "My brother, choose again." Note how His voice sounds in your mind. What effect does this have on you?

3. Sentence 4 contains a visual image. What word in the sentence alerts you to this fact?

4. The image is an "altar unto joy." What exactly is an altar unto joy?

5. What does this image of an altar to joy symbolize?

6. Now visualize yourself as an altar dedicated to joy. You might use this passage for inspiration: "you will see an altar to your Father, holy as Heaven, glowing with radiant purity and sparkling with the shining lilies you laid upon it" (T-20.VIII.4:4).

7. Read the following passage and collect all the visual words and phrases:

> 4. There is no inherent conflict between justice and truth; one is but the first small step in the direction of the other. 5. The path becomes quite different as one goes along. 6. Nor could all the magnificence, the grandeur of the scene and the enormous opening vistas that rise to meet one as the journey continues, be foretold from the outset. 7. Yet even these, whose splendor reaches indescribable heights as one proceeds, fall short indeed of all that wait when the pathway ceases and time ends with it. (M-19.2:4-7)

8. What is this an image of? Try to put the clues together and come up with the whole picture.

9. What idea does the image symbolize?

10. Now visualize the image, while holding in mind what it symbolizes. For our version of this, consult the answer key.

ANSWER KEY

1. No answer needed.

2. No answer needed.

3. "Altar"

4. An altar is a "usually raised structure...on which sacrifices are offered or incense is burned in worship" (*Webster's*). An altar is a raised structure dedicated to some kind of deity. The phrase "altar to God" appears many times in the Course, meaning an altar dedicated to God. "Altar unto joy" therefore refers to an altar dedicated to joy.

5. It symbolizes you. It says that your nature is wholly dedicated to joy. Devotion to joy is what you are.

7. Visual words and phrases: path, grandeur of the scene, enormous opening vistas, indescribable heights, pathway.

8. The image is of a mountain climb. What else could it be? There is a journey on an ascending path that leads you to indescribable heights and lets you see enormous vistas.

9. The image symbolizes the spiritual journey, the journey to God.

10. You begin the journey in a state of injustice, which (according to the section in which this passage occurs) is a state of condemnation towards your brothers. You ultimately decide to leave this state and pursue a higher one; you decide to leave the plains and climb up into the mountains.

The first part of the journey is not very picturesque. You seem to be only feet above the plain of injustice that you left. From here, you have no idea of the magnificence that awaits you. Yet as you climb higher (as you make further spiritual progress), you are greeted with scenes of grandeur you could never have anticipated. You will turn a corner on the path and there will be an enormous opening vista which takes your breath away. As you climb further, the "splendor reaches indescribable heights." You had no idea you could be this happy.

Yet one day you reach the end of the pathway, the summit of the tallest peak. No matter how great the splendor you have known, nothing you have experienced can compare to what awaits you here. Here, on the roof of the world, you step off the path, off the mountain, out of space, and out of time altogether.

Chapter 16

Step III. Application
B. Reading the Passage as Personally Addressing You

This is a technique with many different variations. We will cover several of the variations in detail in a moment, but for now, think about this topic in general: In every way you can, as you read the Course, try to let it speak to you personally.

Why is this important? Because the Course is addressed to you, personally, and needs to be heard that way to be fully appreciated. I (Allen) believe that each of us has been personally selected by God to read and study this Course just as much as Helen and Bill were selected by God to write it down:

> The plan includes very specific contacts to be made for each teacher of God. There are no accidents in salvation. (M-3.1:5–6)

We have been hand-picked by God to study the Course. Its words are addressed to *us, personally*. We need to read them in that way. Often, we take our understanding of some truth and apply it first to others around us, rather than to ourselves. We read, for instance, "Sickness is anger taken out upon the body" (T-28.VI.5:1); then we tell our friends, "*You* need to stop projecting your anger on your body," instead of recognizing first the ways in which *we* are projecting our anger onto our own bodies. If we will take care of our own diseased thinking, our brothers and sisters will take care of their own. The healing of our mind will spill over into theirs.

"The alertness of the ego to the errors of other egos is not the kind of vigilance the Holy Spirit would have you maintain" (T-9.III.1:1), the Course tells us. If we use the Course to improve our ability to spot errors in other people, we are practicing the wrong kind of vigilance; we need to consistently apply it to ourselves. The way we bring healing to the world is by allowing ourselves to be healed; that is a central theme in the Course:

When I am healed, I am not healed alone.

> And as you let yourself be healed, you see all those around you, or who cross your mind, or whom you touch or those who seem to have no contact with you, healed along with you. (W-pI.137.Title, 10:1)

So, when we read the Course, let's take it as personally addressing us because that is just how it is intended to be taken.

Example 1:

Take those very words above: "When I am healed, I am not healed alone." Make them personal. Emphasize the "I" as you read them aloud. "When *I* am healed, *I* am not healed alone."

Example 2:

> The grace of God rests gently on forgiving eyes, and everything they look on speaks of Him to the beholder. He can see no evil; nothing in the world to fear, and no one who is different from himself. (T-25.VI.1:1–2)

These lines are written in a generic way, as is much of the Course. Read them as addressing you personally. Make them be about you. Paraphrase it in your mind, perhaps: "The grace of God will rest gently on my eyes when I forgive, and everything my eyes look on will speak of God to me. I will see no evil; nothing in the world to fear; and no one who is different from me."

Here are some of the specific ways in which we can read the Course's words as speaking to us personally:

i. Engage in a dialogue with the author

As you read, mentally talk back to the author; to Jesus, if naming him does not bother you at this point. For instance, when he says, "Hear me, my brothers, hear and join with me" (T-31.VIII.9:4), you can respond: "I hear you, brother Jesus, and I now choose to join with you."

When he says, "Would you behold your brother? God is glad to have you look on him" (T-25.VI.3:2–3), you can dialogue:

> "Would you behold your brother?"
> *"Yes, I would behold my brother."*
> "God is glad to have you look on him."
> *"I'm glad to know that, and glad to look on him, too."*

Sometimes, such dialoguing can take the form of questions. You may read something that you don't understand. If you give voice to your question, which might be, "What do you mean by that, Jesus?" you may find that, in the lines that follow, your mind will find the answer that much more quickly.

I find that frequently reminding myself that I am reading the words of a very present teacher, one who is looking over my shoulder ready to help, as it were, makes me much more open to the present guidance and instruction of God's Voice within.

ii. Put what you are reading into first person form

Often, when the author of the Course wants some material to really sink in and become our own, he puts it in first person form, making it read as if we ourselves are the author of these words. One can see this especially in the Workbook. There, the six reviews, as well as Part II, are all filled with material in the first person. This fits the goal of the Workbook reviews, which is this: Having practiced a lesson once, we are now going to practice it again to truly make it a part of us. Putting the material in the first person suits this purpose perfectly, for now it sounds as if these are our own thoughts. For this same reason, the lessons in Part II of the Workbook are almost entirely in first person. This is the part of the Workbook where we are supposed to really claim the ideas as our own. What better way to facilitate this than to write them down as if they *are* our own?

Review I is a perfect example of this first person usage in the Workbook. There, we are instructed to spend time thinking about the lessons we are reviewing. We are then given a paragraph for each lesson which reads as if it consists of our own thoughts about that lesson. Here is an example:

60. (47) **God is the strength in which I trust.**

It is not my own strength through which I forgive.
It is through the strength of God in me, which I am remembering as I forgive.
As I begin to see, I recognize His reflection on earth.
I forgive all things because I feel the stirring of His strength in me.
And I begin to remember the Love I chose to forget, but Which has not forgotten me.

We have placed the above sentences on separate lines to help us read them in the intended way. So let's do that now. Go back over the above paragraph very slowly, dwelling on each word and each sentence. Most of all, read these thoughts as if you are the one thinking them. When you come to words denoting yourself ("I," "me," "mine"), give them special emphasis in your mind.

How did that feel? One can casually read over such material and receive no benefit at all. Then, a moment later, one can read the same material again with a different mental approach, and feel transported.

It is clear that the author of the Course feels that putting things in first person form has value. We, therefore, should feel full permission to do this ourselves with any of the Course's material. It really can transform something that seems at first to be dry or abstract into something rich and full of life.

Example 1:

Take this passage:

> For you *will* hear, and you *will* choose again. And in this choice is everyone made free. (T-31.VIII.9:6–7)

Now put it into the first person:

For I *will* hear, and I *will* choose again. And in this choice I am made free.

Example 2:

It works with longer passages, also. Compare these two passages:

> The journey that we undertake together is the exchange of dark for light, of ignorance for understanding. Nothing you understand is fearful. It is only in darkness and in ignorance that you perceive the frightening, and shrink away from it to further darkness. And yet it is only the hidden that can terrify, not for what it is, but for its hiddenness. The obscure is frightening because you do not understand its meaning. If you did, it would be clear and you would be no longer in the dark. Nothing has hidden value, for what is hidden cannot be shared, and so its value is unknown. The hidden is kept apart, but value always lies in joint appreciation. What is concealed cannot be loved, and so it must be feared. (T-14.VI.1:1–9)

In the journey that I am undertaking with Jesus, I am exchanging dark for light, and ignorance for understanding. Nothing that I understand is fearful [i.e. If I understand something I am not afraid of it]. It is only in darkness and in ignorance that I perceive the frightening, and I shrink away from it to further darkness. And yet only the hidden can terrify me, not because of what it is, but because of its hiddenness. The obscure is frightening because I do not understand its meaning. If I did, it would be clear and I would be no longer in the dark. Nothing has hidden value, for I cannot share what is hidden, and so its value is unknown. The hidden is kept apart, but value always lies in joint appreciation [appreciation that I am sharing with someone else]. When I conceal something I cannot love it, and so I must fear it.

Just changing the words around like that can make a passage that seemed at first difficult or uninteresting into something very relevant to your daily life. "Only the hidden can terrify me." The notion that things are frightening to us, not because of what they are, but simply because of their hiddenness, starts to look very practical to me, and encourages me to bring everything into the light.

iii. Turn what you are reading into a prayer

This is one of my favorite techniques. It's one that really works wonders for me. I think that it would be interesting to take some of that same paragraph above and apply the technique to it. I have not done it before with that paragraph, so the results will be spontaneous. I'm not picking the paragraph because it lends itself particularly well to the technique; I'm hoping this will show it can work with nearly anything.

> *Father, I'm on a journey in which I am exchanging dark for light, and ignorance for understanding. I thank You that I have a companion on this journey; someone is taking this journey with me. Jesus is assisting me to give up my ignorance, and to take his understanding. I am glad to bring things out of the dark, into the light, where they can be seen and thus understood. Truly, Father, when I see something I can understand it, and when I understand it I'm not afraid of it. Jesus, help me to let this realization truly*

sink in, so that I am less afraid of bringing the dark things into the light; help me to understand how much this helps me on my journey. Help me to realize that the journey consists in exchanging the dark for the light.

When I practice this technique, my prayers are not quite so flowing as that. Sometimes I just repeat a few words over and over, until the Holy Spirit infuses them with some kind of light. I might say, for instance, "Dark for light. Dark for light. Yes, I am exchanging dark for light. I want to get rid of the dark. I want to welcome the light. Dark for light."

Remember, no one is listening to you except God. Nobody is going to grade you on your prayers. So just let them flow however you like. Laugh, cry, sing. One thing I do sometimes is to pray aloud while I am driving. I will bring some sentence from the Course to mind, and then start to turn it over and over in my mind, "Dark for light, dark for light," like I did above. I have been known even to shout as I drive down the highway! One day I took the phrase from the Workbook, "My Father gives all power unto me" (W-pII.320). I let myself get really excited. I would have fit right in to a group that was speaking in tongues; I was shouting, "All power! Wow! *All* power. And *unto me!* Unbelievable! Unto me!" Suddenly I realized I was at a traffic light, and the lady in the car next to me was giving me a very strange and somewhat fearful stare! It was a bit embarrassing. But I figure the benefits are worth the minor embarrassment. Besides, those other drivers don't know me anyhow.

You don't have to get that crazy, of course. Just take the words of the Course and turn them into prayer, in whatever way fits your fancy, whatever feels comfortable to you. Do it aloud, do it silently, do it in writing; it doesn't matter. It's a great way to get the words of the Course engaged with your own life.

iv. *Insert your name in appropriate places*

One very effective way of making a passage come alive for you personally is the very simple technique of reading it to yourself and inserting your own name at appropriate places. You might think that such an obvious, mechanical technique would not have a lot of effect, but give it a try. I find that it often has startling results for me.

Example 1:

Let's take as an example the first paragraph of Chapter 3, Section II, "Miracles as True Perception." First, read through the paragraph as written:

> I have stated that the basic concepts referred to in this course are not matters of degree. Certain fundamental concepts cannot be understood in terms of opposites. It is impossible to conceive of light and darkness or everything and nothing as joint possibilities. They are all true or all false. It is essential that you realize your thinking will be erratic until a firm commitment to one or the other is made. A firm commitment to darkness or nothingness, however, is impossible. No one has ever lived who has not experienced *some* light and *some* thing. No one, therefore, is able to deny truth totally, even if he thinks he can. (T-3.II.1:1-8)

The paragraph is quite strong as written, admittedly, but with a little minor rewriting to insert your own name, it becomes very powerful and very affecting. I will use my own name here, but try reading it aloud substituting your name for mine:

> I have stated that the basic concepts referred to in this course are not matters of degree. Certain fundamental concepts, Allen, cannot be understood in terms of opposites. It is impossible for you to conceive of light and darkness or everything and nothing as joint possibilities. They are all true or all false. Allen, it is essential that you realize your thinking will be erratic until you, Allen, make a firm commitment to one or the other. A firm commitment to darkness or nothingness, however, is impossible. No one has ever lived – and that includes you, Allen – who has not experienced *some* light and *some* thing. You, Allen, therefore, cannot deny truth totally, even if you think you can.

I find that when I read the paragraph in this way, when it gets to that part about making a firm commitment to darkness or to light, I start feeling nervous. Then, when it goes on to say that a firm commitment to darkness is *impossible*, and that I cannot deny truth totally even if I think I can, I feel an enormous sense of relief. And it is very clear to me: I am going to find my own thinking to be erratic until I make a firm commitment to light and to truth, but I don't have to worry that I am going to become totally blinded. There are really only two possibilities: confusion (in which I am trying to hold on to both light and darkness), and total clarity (when I decide 100 percent for the light).

Example 2:

Putting my own name in there just brings it home for me.

Let's do just one more short example, taken from the same section. Here's the original sentence:

> Nothing can prevail against a Son of God who commends his spirit into the Hands of his Father.
>
> (T-3.II.5:1)

As written, that is a warmly reassuring statement. Put your own name into it and it becomes a personal promise from God to you:

> Nothing can prevail against a Son of God like you, Allen, when you commend your spirit into the Hands of your Father.

If you are a woman and find it difficult, as many women do, to relate to being called a "Son" of God, you may want to change the word "Son" to "Child." I personally do not think it is a good idea to substitute "daughter" here, because – in my mind, at least – that tends to emphasize gender differences rather than minimize them. But I am a man, at least my bodily form is, so perhaps I can't relate to how this feels for some women. If using feminine words brings the truth closer to home for you, then go for it! That is the whole idea behind personal application.

I have had a few women tell me that they prefer keeping the words the Course uses, and referring to themselves as "the Son of God." They say it is personally meaningful to them because it makes it clear to them that their physical gender has no effect whatsoever on the nature of their relationship with God. They, although women, are just as much "the Son of God" as I am, or as Jesus is. So, as I have said already, use the words that bring the truth home to *you*.

v. Respond to instructions that are given

This is one of those points that, when I go to put it into writing, makes me feel as though you, the reader, are going to say to me, "Du-uh! Golly gee, I would have never thought of that – NOT! How dumb do you think we are?" The only thing that encourages me to go ahead to state the very obvious is the knowledge that I sometimes overlook it myself. If *I* do, I figure maybe you do sometimes, as well.

What is this obvious point I'm talking about? Just this:

> When the Course actually tells you to do something specific, *do* it.

See what I mean? That's a pretty obvious idea, isn't it? But let me give you some examples of how I have, in the past, overlooked the obvious, and how I have found that taking new note of the obvious, and doing what the Course tells me to do, has really revolutionized my life.

Example 1:

Take these familiar lines from the Text:

> When you are sad, *know this need not be.* Depression comes from a sense of being deprived of something you want and do not have. Remember that you are deprived of nothing except by your own decisions, and then decide otherwise. (T-4.IV.3:1-3)

How many times, when I have been sad, have I ignored these lines? How about you? Have you caught hold of your thoughts of sadness and told yourself, "This need not be"? Have you consciously and deliberately recalled that you cannot be deprived of anything except by your own decisions –

and then decided otherwise?

Example 2:

I realized how little I actually paid attention to what the Text was telling me to do when, not too long ago, Robert handed out a paper to our local class of specific *practices* that are presented to us in the Text. These are passages like the above that tell us, for instance:

When your peace is threatened or disturbed in any way,
say to yourself:

> *I do not know what anything, including this, means.*
> *And so I do not know how to respond to it.*
> *And I will not use my own past learning as the light to guide me now.* (T-14.XI.6:6-9)

That is an extremely powerful practice. It is one that is meant to be used, to be actually memorized and repeated whenever we feel our peace threatened or disturbed. Robert's paper listed more than two dozen of such practices, and you know what? Most of them I had never practiced! Not once! I have read those passages maybe dozens of times, and never once did I actually do what the Text was telling me to do.

I decided to start trying to do what the Text tells me to do when I read it. When I read a passage like that, now, I stop, see if I am aware of anything in my life that seems to be threatening or disturbing my peace, and then do the practice. (I almost never fail to find *something* that is threatening my peace!) Finding something threatening my peace is just what this passage addresses; other passages address other things.

It isn't just the practices, however, that the Text asks us to do. Sometimes it asks us to interact with itself as we read. It asks us to think about something. It asks us questions, expecting us to think about the answer before going on. Just doing that sort of thing can bring the passage to life.

Example 3:

At times, it even goes into guided meditations. Have you ever followed these instructions from Chapter 13?:

> Sit quietly and look upon the world you see, and tell yourself: "The real world is not like this. It has no buildings and there are no streets where people walk alone and separate. There are no stores where people buy an endless list of things they do not need. It is not lit with artificial light, and night comes not upon it. There is no day that brightens and grows dim. There is no loss. Nothing is there but shines, and shines forever."
>
> (T-13.VII.1:1-7)

Try it! When you find yourself reading some kind of instruction in the Text, *just do it.* You will be amazed at the results, and at how much more understanding you gain of the passage.

vi. Read it as if Jesus is talking to you

If the Course is speaking to you, there must be a speaker. As all students know, the Course claims that this speaker is Jesus. If you can accept that claim (and we believe that accepting it is a very personal thing that no one can force upon another), the words of the Course can take on added significance and impact for you. Our reaction to anything said to us is based not only on *what* is said, it is also based on our opinion of *who* is saying it. We always, as the saying goes, "consider the source." For most of us, if we really believe that the Course comes from Jesus, its words will carry far more authority in our minds than they would have otherwise. This gives those words greater ability to transform our thinking.

You can heighten this effect. First, you can consciously remember that Jesus is the one speaking these words. You can hold this awareness in your mind. Second, you can imagine him speaking these words to you personally, rather than to a general readership or to the air. If the Course is your intended path, then, in a sense, he did speak these words to you. Further, the Course teaches that he is with you very personally at all times. You thus might imagine him repeating the words with you as you read them, just as he says he will repeat with you the words of the Workbook lessons as you practice them:

> Together we review these thoughts [the central thoughts of the Workbook lessons]. Together we devote our time and effort to them. (W-pI.rV.IN.8:2-3)

This is most easily done with the material in which Jesus speaks in the first person. Most of this is found in the first twenty chapters of the Text. There is also some in the Workbook, however: in Review V and in many of the lessons in Part II. Watch for this material as you read. Watch for the author referring to himself directly as "I" or "me." When you come across such material, focus on it. Hear it as if Jesus is speaking it directly to you.

Reading the Course as if Jesus is speaking it to you, however, need not be confined to these parts. You can do this with any part of the Course. To enhance this, feel free to occasionally fill in "my brother" or "my child" – Jesus' favorite ways of addressing us in the Course. But you can fill in whatever you want: "my friend," "my sister," "my student," "my disciple," "my fellow Son of God." For instance: "You *are* as God created you, my dear friend, and so is every living thing you look upon" (based on T-31.VIII.6).

Reading the Course with this mind-set can transform the experience. Instead of being a dry exercise of reading abstract ideas on a page, it can become a living relationship in which your teacher takes you by the hand and leads you home.

Exercise in reading the passage as personally addressing you

For this exercise we will again use Paragraph 3 of "Choose Once Again":

> 1. Trials are but lessons that you failed to learn presented once again, so where you made a faulty choice before you now can make a better one, and thus escape all pain that what you chose before has brought to you. 2. In every difficulty, all distress, and each perplexity Christ calls to you and gently says, "My brother, choose again." 3. He would not leave one source of pain unhealed, nor any image left to veil the truth. 4. He would remove all misery from you whom God created altar unto joy. 5. He would not leave you comfortless, alone in dreams of hell, but would release your mind from everything that hides His face from you. 6. His holiness is yours because He is the only Power that is real in you. 7. His strength is yours because He is the Self That God created as His only Son.   (T-31.VIII.3)

1. Since the main figure in this paragraph aside from you is

Christ, your true Self, try having a dialogue with Him. Read Sentence 2 slowly. Hear Christ calling to you. What do you want to say back to Him in response?

Now go on to Sentence 3. Take seriously that He wants to remove all sources of pain from you, that He wants to bring you face-to-face with the joyous, eternal truth. Again, what do you want to say to Him in response?

Go on and do this with the remaining sentences in this paragraph. How did you find the experience? What sorts of things did you say to Christ? Did you express gratitude? Affirm your willingness to follow Him? Ask questions? Is this the kind of thing you would benefit from doing more often?

2. Read the above paragraph slowly, changing it into first person form. Change "you" and "yours" into "I," "me" and "mine." Put special emphasis on these words in your mind. Really make the paragraph a statement about you personally.

3. Let's take the first sentence of our paragraph and turn it into a prayer. Read the sentence over slowly, one phrase at a time, and see what your heart wants to say to God. See if a prayer doesn't arise out of you sparked by this sentence. You might find yourself thanking God for repeating your lessons again and again. You might find yourself telling God, like one might tell a bartender, how many faulty choices you have made. You might ask His help to make a better choice. But there is no one right prayer here. Listen inside yourself and see what *you* want to say to God.

4. Read the version of the paragraph below, inserting your name at the indicated places. See if it makes the paragraph more alive for you.

> 1. Trials are but lessons that you failed to learn, [name], presented once again, so where you made a faulty choice before you now can make a better one, and thus escape all pain that what you chose before has brought to you. 2. In every difficulty, all distress, and each perplexity Christ calls to you, [name], and gently says, "My brother, choose again"....5. He would not leave you comfortless, [name], alone in dreams of hell, but would release your mind from everything that hides His face from you. 6. His holiness is yours, [name], because He is the only Power that is real in you.

5. Now read the above passage again, this time imagining that Jesus is speaking it personally to you. At the points where it says "[name]," you might either imagine Jesus saying your name, or imagine him calling you "my child," "my brother," "my sister," or "my friend."

6. Sentence 2 contains an instruction. Christ is telling you, in every trying circumstance, to choose again. Try carrying out this instruction. Think of a difficulty, distress or perplexity currently in your life. Now realize that the way you have been looking at this situation keeps you locked into pain, and into repetition of the same basic pattern. Realize also that Christ is calling to you in that very situation. Here Him saying, "My brother, choose again." Now choose whether you would see yourself as a weak body, put upon by the world, or see yourself as the Son of God, who is still as God created you.

Chapter 17

Step III. Application
C. Identifying in Yourself Thoughts or States of Mind the Course Speaks About

So often that it is practically a signature of his writing style, Jesus presumes to tells us what we are thinking or what we believe. Often this is quite overt. The phrase "you believe," for instance, occurs 212 times; the phrase "you think" occurs 281 times. In other instances it is less obvious, but if you read carefully, you quickly realize that the author is claiming to describe the thought processes of your own mind. And if you will examine your mind when you notice this, you will find that he is uncannily accurate in his assessment of our minds.

This application technique has two parts:

- *recognizing when the author is referring to your own patterns of thought*
- *seeking to identify or locate the thought patterns he speaks of in your own mind*

The reason this technique is so useful is that when the

author points out something about the way we think, he has a reason for doing so. Usually, he wants us to see how foolish or insane our thoughts really are, so that we will choose to let them go. He often points out that unless we look closely at our errors, and see through to their illusory nature, we won't let them go: "No one can escape from illusions unless he looks at them, for not looking is the way they are protected" (T-11.V.1:1). Thus, the reason Jesus bothers to tell us what we are thinking is because *we have not noticed!* He tells us because he wants to make sure we do notice, so that our insane thoughts can be looked at and undone.

Not only have we *not* noticed, we don't *want* to notice. The Course has a habit of pointing out things in our mind that we just don't want to see. We see ourselves as sincere spiritual seekers. God is our goal in life. We have been on the path for years. And besides that, we are nice people. When the Course talks about our attraction to guilt, about our worshipping of the corpse of death on the throne of God, about our desire to rob other people until nothing is left to steal, about our ego's murderous impulses, surely it must be talking about someone else!

The Course is trying hard to take the smiling disguise off of our ego. That disguise is worn by everyone, whether on the spiritual path or off. Yet once we step on the path, this disguise, rather than being discarded, usually dons a set of white robes. Our now serene, wise, and holy disguise becomes our substitute for real spiritual advancement. But a substitute is not the real thing, and when we find that we are not truly happy, that our peace is still fragile, we wonder why. We secretly suspect that, since we have held up our end so well, God must be lagging on His.

We are not going to make that real spiritual progress until we are willing to look at the ugliness that is actually inside our minds. It is the hidden source of our pain, and until it goes, our suffering will stay. Therefore, we *want* to find the things that Jesus is talking about in our minds. We want to uncover them. They are there; they are causing us pain; so let's dig them up and get rid of them.

Assuming that the ugliness is there inside of us is a crucial part of this technique. It helps to remember that Jesus is not describing thoughts that exist in some people and not in others. He is describing various aspects of a thought system that everyone carries. The ego is like a computer program. Different users may customize their program, or use it slightly differently, but they still have the same program. In telling us what we believe, Jesus is simply talking about different functions of the program that we all purchased. Therefore, as long as you still believe in the ego – as long as you experience yourself as an individual entity – you still own the whole program. Your investment in the program will decrease over time. You will rely on it less and use it less often. But until you drag it into the trash, it's still there on your hard drive – all of it.

So when you come across the Course talking about some dark thought in your mind, try to remind yourself that this thought is simply part of the ego program. Everyone has it – you included. And until you find it and root it out, it will continue weighing you down and sapping your strength. You can profit greatly, therefore, from examining your mind with ruthless honesty to see if you can find that thought in you.

Example 1:

The first instance of "you believe" in the Text is in its very first section: "You believe that what your physical eyes cannot see does not exist" (T-1.I.22:2). Even as we read this now, we probably think of these words as applying to someone else. Not to us, surely! We "know" that the body is only an illusion, that the body's eyes cannot see the inner altar (T-2.III.1:10). We "know" quite well that our reality is spirit, even though that reality is invisible to our physical eyes. Don't we? Or do we?

If we are honest with ourselves, we will realize that this sentence is true of us to a greater or lesser degree, but true *in some degree:* We do believe that what our physical eyes cannot see does not exist. Most of the time, this is how we think. Most of the time, although we may give lip service to the spiritual world that is invisible to our body's eyes, we act as if it were not there. We claim to believe that the Holy Spirit is with us at all times, guiding us, and yet we seldom speak to Him and even more seldom listen to Him. We devote most of our time and attention to caring for things the body's eyes *can* see, and very little time to caring for what our eyes do not see. We are far more likely to skip our quiet time than to skip our breakfast.

Oh, we do believe that what our physical eyes cannot see really exists – sometimes. But that belief is, as yet, far from a settled certainty. And yes, there will come a day when, finally, these words will no longer be true of us, when we have learned to trust in the reality of "the real world" of which the Course speaks; that day is in fact the goal of the Course. It aims to rid our minds of false beliefs. Yet until that day has come, it is vital to admit to ourselves just how invested we are in the belief that our eyes disclose what is real and important.

What I (Allen) just did as I wrote this is a demonstration of the technique I am writing about. I have been looking for ways in which I actually do think the thought that Jesus says I hold, even when at first I may not think I think it. I have been searching my own mind for evidence that this disbelief in what my eyes cannot see is actually there. Applying the Course in this way isn't always easy. Our egos are very well protected. Such rooting around in our mental basement isn't attractive; we might find spider webs, or even spiders, or – yuk! – rats!

This technique is one way we can carry out the frequent admonition the Course gives us to look within. Probably the biggest reason we don't do it is because we are afraid of what we might find:

> Do not be afraid to look within. The ego tells you all is black with guilt within you, and bids you not to look. Instead, it bids you look upon your brothers, and see the guilt in them. Yet this you cannot do without remaining blind. For those who see their brothers in the dark, and guilty in the dark in which they shroud them, are too afraid to look upon the light within. Within you is not what you believe is there, and what you put your faith in. Within you is the holy sign of perfect faith your Father has in you. (T-13.IX.8:1–7)

When we look inside ourselves with profound honesty, we will initially see the ugliness. Yet our honesty will allow us to see the darkness as a facade, an illusion. We will eventually look past it and gaze upon our perfect innocence, unsullied by the darkest thought we ever entertained. This is the ultimate goal of identifying in ourselves the thoughts the Course speaks about.

Example 2:

> No one who comes here but must still have hope, some lingering illusion, or some dream that there is something outside of himself that will bring happiness and peace to him. (T-29.VII.2:1)

The "here" we are coming to is the world. So Jesus is saying that everyone who comes to this world has some "hope, some lingering illusion, or some dream that there is something outside of himself that will bring happiness and peace." That means he is saying that *I* have such hopes, illusions and dreams. Let me first notice that he is referring here to *my thinking*.

Then, as the second part of the process, let me examine my mind to see if that thought pattern exists in me. Do I have some hope of finding something outside myself that will bring me happiness?

We doubt there is a single one of us who can ask himself or herself that question without responding, "Wow! Do I ever!" We might even want to make a mental list of a few of the things we have thought would bring happiness or peace in the past, and then think of some of the things we still, to this day, have lingering illusions about. If we pause and do this kind of thinking, then the material next to this passage will have far greater personal impact:

> Seek not outside yourself. For it will fail, and you will weep each time an idol falls. Heaven cannot be found

> where it is not, and there can be no peace excepting there. Each idol that you worship when God calls will never answer in His place. There is no other answer you can substitute, and find the happiness His answer brings. Seek not outside yourself. For all your pain comes simply from a futile search for what you want, insisting where it must be found. What if it is not there? Do you prefer that you be right or happy? Be you glad that you are told where happiness abides, and seek no longer elsewhere. You will fail. But it is given you to know the truth, and not to seek for it outside yourself.
>
> (T-29.VII.1:1–12)

When I realize that these words are speaking directly to me, addressing a very relevant situation that exists right now in my life and my mind, how powerful they become! How stirring their message is to me! To think: All my pain comes simply from a futile search for what I want, insisting it must be found outside of myself! And I can see myself doing that very thing! I am participating in this vain program because I secretly believe I am not whole within, and so I fear to look within, certain that if I do I will find devastation. I do believe that foolish lie, but I no longer want to. I choose, in this moment, to change, to choose to look within, past the illusion of sin and guilt, to catch a glimpse of the radiant Son of God at the center of my very being. *This* is who I am! *This* is where I can find happiness and peace in truth!

There may be no more powerful application technique in the study of the Course than this one. It guides us directly into one of the core spiritual practices taught by the Course, which is looking at the ego within our own minds, bringing our ego thoughts into the presence of the Holy Spirit and truth, where they are found wanting, and finally, choosing to let this insanity go. We warmly, and with great love, recommend to all Course students to put as much effort as they can into learning and practicing this technique.

> The Holy Spirit asks of you but this; bring to Him every secret you have locked away from Him. Open every door to Him, and bid Him enter the darkness and lighten it away. At your request He enters gladly. He brings the light to darkness if you make the darkness open to Him. But what you hide He cannot look upon. He sees for you, and unless you look with Him He cannot see. The vision of Christ is not for Him alone, but for Him with you. Bring, therefore, all your dark and secret thoughts to Him, and look upon them with Him. He holds the light, and you the darkness. They cannot coexist when Both of You together look on them. His judgment must prevail, and He will give it to you as you join your perception to His. (T-14.VII.6:1–11)

Exercise in identifying in yourself thoughts or states of mind the Course speaks about

For this exercise we are not going to use Paragraph 3 of "Choose Once Again" because it does not lend itself very well to this technique. Instead, we will pull two passages from elsewhere in the Course.

> ...the ego comes to save you. God made you a body. Very well. Let us accept this and be glad. As a body, do not let yourself be deprived of what the body offers. Take the little you can get. God gave you nothing. The body

> is your only savior. It is the death of God and your salvation. (W-pI.72.6:1-9)

1. This paragraph presents how the ego comes to save you. In other words, this is the ego's counsel, not the Course's teaching (as we saw in the second example in Chapter 12). Read this paragraph over again and ask yourself if you have the thoughts or attitudes discussed. Have you ever felt that God, or life, didn't give you very much to be happy about? Has that feeling led you to take refuge in bodily pleasures and comforts, to "take the little you can get"? Have you ever decided that, because of your overall deprivation, you are not going to "let yourself be deprived of what the body offers"?

If so, realize that the last two lines are beliefs in your mind as well. Somewhere in your mind you believe that the body is your savior from the nothingness bequeathed you by God. You, therefore, must procure for yourself the happiness God never granted you, and jilt Him for another source of happiness. Your body is thus your substitute for God. It is an implicit statement that you don't need God or His way of salvation. It represents the death of God in your life. These are not easy beliefs to face, but they flow directly from the idea that your body gives you the happiness that God didn't.

> What is this precious thing, this priceless pearl, this hidden secret treasure, to be wrested in righteous wrath from this most treacherous and cunning enemy? It must be what you want but never found. And now you "understand" the reason why you found it not. For it was taken from you by this enemy, and hidden where you would not think to look. He hid it in his body, making it the cover for his guilt, the hiding place for what

belongs to you. Now must his body be destroyed and sacrificed, that you may have that which belongs to you. His treachery demands his death, that you may live. And you attack only in self-defense. (T-23.II.11:2-9)

2. Read this passage over and see if you can identify these thoughts in your mind, at least at some point in time. Have you ever felt that another person had what you want but never found? Have you felt that this person held the priceless pearl, the secret treasure that could make your life complete, but that he or she refused to give it to you? Did you feel that, in a sense, this person had taken – even *stolen* – what was rightfully yours? Did you feel that this treasure lay hidden in this person's body, like a jewel in a vault? And did you ever have thoughts of doing violence to that body, in order to forcibly take ownership of that hidden treasure? And, while having those thoughts, did you feel that this violence would in some sense be justified – an understandable case of self-defense against the terrible injustice done to you?

Chapter 18

Step III. Application
D. Applying What You Are Reading to the Specifics of Your Life

Applying what we are reading to the specifics of our lives is perhaps the summit of Course study. Everything we have done thus far leads us to this point. We have observed so that we can interpret, and we have interpreted so that we can apply. We cannot apply until we understand (at least to some degree) what we are reading. Yet until we apply, the purpose of what we are reading has not been fulfilled. This final technique is not the only application technique, of course. But it is the place where we apply the material directly to our lives – to our needs, problems and concerns, as Review III in the Workbook says. This is the place where the lofty principles of the Course meet the specific situations, events, and people of our lives. This is where application reaches most fully into where we live.

The Course's theory has only one purpose: to be put into practice in our lives. Two quotes in particular state this with particular clarity:

> This is not a course in the play of ideas, but in their practical application. (T-11.VIII.5:3)

> This is the year for the application of the ideas that have been given you. For the ideas are mighty forces, to be used and not held idly by. (T-16.II.9:4-5)

This relationship between theory and practice is also the relationship between Text and Workbook. The Text provides the theoretical application; the Workbook provides the practical application, without which the goal of the Course is not attainable (W-In.1:2). Yet this same relationship exists inside the Text. The Text itself contains both theory and practice. The Text contains numerous practices – lines we are instructed to repeat whenever we feel threatened, afraid, upset, etc.

Further, Text sections regularly lay down theory and then, in the last couple of paragraphs, end on a note of practical application. They ask us to apply the theory we've just been given. With a section, you can spot this switch from theory to application when injunctions start appearing, when the material starts saying, in essence, "do this." For example, here is how the last paragraph of "The Secret Vows" opens: "Let this be your agreement with each one; that you be one with him and not apart" (T-28.VI.6:1). That is an injunction. It is telling you to do something, to take the teaching contained in that section and apply it.

The Text itself, then, is meant to be practical. In fact, the Course tells us that if we made full use of the Text, we wouldn't even need the Workbook (see W-pI.39.2:5-6)! We are supposed to be reading the Text and constantly applying what we read to our lives. Many students think of the early Text sections as especially dry and theoretical, but Jesus felt differently. Early in the dictation of the Text he urged Helen and Bill to study "the notes" (the Course material) and then explained why: "Neither of you realizes that many of the problems you keep being faced with may *already* have been solved there" (*Absence from Felicity*, p. 258). So Helen and Bill were supposed to study the Course *in order* to find in it the solutions to their recurring problems. And that is what we, too, are supposed to do.

One example should be enough to make plain how effective this can be. As I (Allen) was preparing for the recent launch of our Electronic Text Class, in which we are sending via electronic mail a weekly commentary on the Text to over 300 subscribers, I began to be apprehensive. As one colleague put it to me, "You have signed up for a seven-year contract with weekly deadlines!" I think you can understand how I might have begun to wonder what I had agreed to! Was I up to it? Could I write a meaningful commentary once a week for 39 weeks of the year, for the next nearly seven years? I began to doubt myself, to be afraid that I would screw up somehow. Some time in that next seven years I was almost certain to experience at least one bout of depression, at least one week of rebellion where I just didn't want to write! How could I have been so stupid as to agree to do this? And now we had a whole bunch of people who had paid in advance for commentaries I had not even written yet. I had to produce, whether or not I felt like it. I was suddenly terrified!

As part of that work, I was studying Section III of Chapter 1 in the Text, where I found these words:

> I am the only one who can perform miracles indiscriminately, because I am the Atonement. You have a role in the Atonement which I will dictate to you. Ask me which miracles you should perform. This spares you needless effort, because you will be acting under direct communication. (T-1.III.4:1-4)

I read that as addressing me personally. Jesus was telling me that he was in charge (in the first sentence of the section, in fact, he said it plainly: "I am in charge of the process of Atonement"). I do not have to worry. I have a role to play, yes, but he will dictate it to me. He will tell me exactly what to do. I will be "acting under direct communication." Now, I'm not trying to use that to claim word-for-word divine inspiration for my commentaries, don't misunderstand me. What those words gave me, however, was a profound sense of being taken care of, of being carried along and helped, of being guided by the Guy who is in charge of the whole thing. I will not have to expend "needless effort."

A bit earlier in the section, Jesus says:

> As you share my unwillingness to accept error in yourself and others, you must join the great crusade to correct it; listen to my voice, learn to undo error and act to correct it. The power to work miracles belongs to you. I will provide the opportunities to do them, but you must be ready and willing. Doing them will bring conviction in the ability, because conviction comes through accomplishment. (T-1.III.1:6-9)

Applying that to myself personally, and to my specific situation, I could see that all I really need to do is to listen to Jesus' voice and do as he directs. I have the power to work miracles. I may not know it, I may not *feel* like I have miraculous powers, but I do. Jesus provides the opportunities for me to work miracles; I just need to be ready and willing. As the miracles take place, *then* my conviction in my ability to do them is formed. "Conviction comes through accomplishment." In other words, the way I learn that I can do miracles is *by doing them.* I don't have to be convinced I can do them before I do them; in fact, it is doing them that convinces me!

So, in this project, I may be doubtful of my ability to perform, but Jesus says I have the power I need. If he has told me to do it, I can do it. Come to think of it, he says exactly that later in the Text:

> You are not asked to do mighty tasks yourself. You are merely asked to do the little He suggests you do, trusting Him only to the small extent of believing that, if He asks it, you can do it. You will see how easily all that He asks can be accomplished. (T-14.VII.5:13-15)

So, as I trust him to that "small extent," I will see how easily it will all be accomplished. Does that make the Text relevant to me? It sure does! I think you can see from this example how this sort of personal application can make the Course really come to life for you. I urge you to try it!

How to apply passages to our lives

So how do you apply a passage to the specifics of your life? When you read, simply hold in mind the intention of applying this material to your life. Then, be on the lookout for passages that lend themselves to specific application. When you find such a passage, pick a situation in your life to which to apply it. Here, for instance, is one such passage from the Manual:

> This time ask yourself whether your judgment or the
> Word of God is more likely to be true. (M-11.2:2)

Almost all of us have situations in which we know that our view is different from God's view. This passage, therefore, can readily be applied to our lives. Think of some situation in your life where you are aware that your view and God's are at variance. Maybe you are resisting something you have been genuinely guided to do. Perhaps you are holding onto resentment when you know that God is asking you to forgive. Now ask yourself: Who is more likely to be right here? Given your track record and given Who God is, do you really think you stand a chance of seeing farther and more clearly than Him? Use this question to help you let go of your view. Something in you already wants to let it go. See the fact that God knows better as *permission* to do so. It's OK to let it go. After all, He is God. He *must* be right.

A great place to use this technique is in those passages that talk about "your brother." Whenever you come across one of these, pick a particular person in your life. Then read the passage as if it was written specifically about that person.

So we have outlined three steps here:

1. As you read, look for passages that can readily be applied to your life.
2. Once you spot one, think of a specific situation in your life to which the passage applies.
3. Then simply apply the passage to that situation.

Another way to use this technique is to already have a situation in mind when you go to read the Course. Pick some person or situation that is troubling you, that you want to see differently. Then, open the Course with the intention to apply everything you read to that person or situation.

This practice can be genuinely transformative. Recently, we put on a retreat focused on forgiving a particular person. One of the most effective exercises we did was to have the participants read "Salvation from Fear" (T-24.VI), applying everything they read very specifically to the person they were trying to forgive. We put each sentence on a separate line and inserted some comments, but essentially people were just reading a section and mentally applying it to a particular person. This may not sound very practical, but some of the major experiences of inner healing occurred during this exercise.

Let's try some of this exercise and see if it brings you benefit. Choose a person you would like to see differently, and apply the following lines to him or her. Try to engage these lines with your whole mind. Read them slowly, drinking in every word. Visualize the images, think about the ideas, imagine the statements as literally true. Above all, apply everything specifically to the person you have chosen:

> Before your brother's holiness the world is still [picture this],
> and peace descends on it [because it looks upon your brother's holiness]
> in gentleness and blessing so complete
> that not one trace of conflict still remains
> to haunt you in the darkness of the night.
> He [name] is your savior from the dreams of fear....
> In him is your assurance God is here, and with you now.
> While he is what he is,
> you can be sure that God is knowable and will be known to you.

Bringing the Course to Life

> For He could never leave His Own creation.
> And the sign that this is so lies in your brother [name],
> offered you that all your doubts about yourself
> may disappear before his holiness.
> [Imagine your doubts about yourself disappearing as you gaze on his holiness.]
>
> (T-24.VI.1-2,4-7)

How the Workbook trains us to do this

Relating what we are reading to the specifics of our lives is actually a form of a practice that the Workbook trains us to do, which is restating thoughts from the Workbook in our own words, and applying them to ourselves and our lives. For example, Lesson 82 takes the thought for the day, "The light of the world brings peace to every mind through my forgiveness," and offers us three *suggestions* for applying the lesson to our lives:

> Suggestions for specific forms for applying this idea are:
> *Let peace extend from my mind to yours,* [name].
> *I share the light of the world with you,* [name].
> *Through my forgiveness I can see this as it is.*
>
> (W-pI.82.2:1-4)

In the introduction to this Review section, the Workbook tells us:

> These [specific forms], however, are merely suggestions. It is not the particular words you use that matter.
>
> (W-pI.rII.in.6:3-4)

In other words, the specific forms given are meant to just show us the way – how to take the thought for the day and adapt it to our own lives. Notice how each of these statements takes one aspect of the original sentence and applies it. Without much effort, you probably can think of another two or three ways you could do the same thing. Likewise, with very little additional effort, you can do this with passages from the Text. Perhaps some parts of the Text will be more difficult to apply personally than the Workbook lessons, but we believe that with a little thought, nearly any line from the Course can be made personally meaningful.

If you would like a little practice in applying Course thoughts to the specifics of your life, we can't recommend anything better than Review II in the Workbook, Lessons 81 to 90. Read these lessons over and study what they are doing. Notice how the thoughts are brought down to some specific situation. A general thought such as, "Let me recognize my problems have been solved," becomes, "I need not wait for *this* to be resolved." That form, of course, is still generic. In real life you can be even more specific: "I don't need to wait until my rent has been paid to be at peace." "The answer to my coming down with the flu is already given to me, if I will accept it." And so on.

If you read over those review lessons you will see that almost every suggested application sentence brings it down to the specific: *this* problem, *this* grievance, some particular person who is *named*, and so on. "This," and "this," and "this," one specific thing after another. Why do you suppose the Workbook spends ten lessons training us to do this kind of application? *Because it is trying to teach us to make a habit of it.*

This form of practice becomes more fully developed in the next review, Review III. Here are the instructions for practice in that review:

> Read over the ideas and comments that are written down for each day's exercise. And then begin to think about them, while letting your mind relate them to your needs, your seeming problems and all your concerns.
> (W-pI.rIII.In.5:2-3)

First, we read over the ideas (the lessons being reviewed) and comments about them. Then we begin to think about the ideas. And, as we do, we let our minds relate the ideas to our needs, problems and concerns. How do we "let" our minds do this? We are given special instruction for this:

> Place the ideas within your mind, and let it use them as it chooses. Give it faith that it will use them wisely, being helped in its decisions by the One Who gave the thoughts to you. What can you trust but what is in your mind? Have faith, in these reviews, the means the Holy Spirit uses [your mind] will not fail. The wisdom of your mind will come to your assistance. Give direction at the outset; then lean back in quiet faith, and let the mind employ the thoughts you gave as they were given you for it to use. (W-pI.rIII.In.6)

We are supposed to simply place the ideas in our minds, having faith that our minds will use the ideas wisely, being aided by the Holy Spirit. Then we "lean back in quiet faith" and let our minds apply the ideas to our needs, problems, and concerns.

For an example, let me (Robert) take the lesson I am practicing today and apply this technique to it. My lesson is 272: "How can illusions satisfy God's Son?" I will place it in my mind, then lean back and let my mind apply it to my needs, problems and concerns:

> I think I can be satisfied by a delicious lunch or a hot shower, but I am God's Son. I am satisfied only by my Father. Only infinity will satisfy me. I think that if I had fewer responsibilities today, if this book were not behind schedule, then I would be at peace. But my responsibilities are illusions. How can any way in which illusions are configured truly satisfy me? In thinking I am satisfied by such paltry things I am selling myself short. I am thinking I am something less than God's boundless Son. I think that if various interpersonal frictions around me today were lessened, then I would be happy. But I know better. Only seeing past the frictions to Who these people really are will make me happy. I am God's Son. No illusion will satisfy me.

You get the point. You just place an idea from the Course in your mind, and then let your mind creatively apply the idea to your current needs, problems and concerns. The thoughts that come out of you feel like they are genuinely your own, yet they often carry a wisdom that seems beyond you. This technique thus becomes a real meeting point of the Course's ideas, the Holy Spirit's inspiration, and your own thoughts. Here, these three become one.

This technique may be a practice from the Workbook, but you can obviously use it with any material in the Course. You could be reading a section in the Text, be struck by a particular sentence, and apply this technique to that sentence.

Notice that this Workbook practice is something we are labeling a study technique. Which is it? Is it study or is it practice? Clearly, the lines between the two have completely blurred here. In this final technique, study *becomes* practice. Reading the Course becomes a spiritual exercise.

Exercise in applying what we read to the specifics of our lives

We will again use Paragraph 3 of "Choose Once Again" for our exercise.

> 1. Trials are but lessons that you failed to learn presented once again, so where you made a faulty choice before you now can make a better one, and thus escape all pain that what you chose before has brought to you. 2. In every difficulty, all distress, and each perplexity Christ calls to you and gently says, "My brother, choose again." 3. He would not leave one source of pain unhealed, nor any image left to veil the truth. 4. He would remove all misery from you whom God created altar unto joy. 5. He would not leave you comfortless, alone in dreams of hell, but would release your mind from everything that hides His face from you. 6. His holiness is yours because He is the only Power that is real in you. 7. His strength is yours because He is the Self That God created as His only Son. (T-31.VIII.3)

1. Sentences 1 and 2 obviously lend themselves to specific application. Think of a situation in your life that fits these sentences. Think of a current trial or difficulty. Now plug this situation into these sentences:

> My trying situation involving_____is but a lesson that I failed to learn presented once again, so where I made a faulty choice before I now can make a

better one, and thus escape all pain that what I chose before has brought to me. In this situation involving_____Christ calls to me and gently says, "My brother, choose again."

Did this cause you to see your situation any differently? Did any new insights come to mind? What choice do you think Christ is asking you to make in this situation?

2. Sentence 3 also lends itself to specific application. Think of a "source of pain," something in your mind that has perhaps plagued you for a long time. Then think of an image you hold of someone, an image that has veiled the truth from your eyes. Perhaps it is an image you hold of someone you resent, or perhaps an image of yourself. You might even want to *match* the image and the source of pain – your pain might involve the person you hold the image of. Now read Sentence 3 while inserting these specifics:

> He would not leave your source of pain [specify] unhealed, nor your image of so-and-so [specify] left to veil the truth.

3. Let us do the same with Sentence 4. Pick a specific misery that you have been carrying and insert it into the sentence:

> He would remove your misery about_____from you whom God created altar unto joy.

4. With Sentence 5, think of some of the perceptions you have that hide the face of Christ from you. This would be almost any perception you carry, perceptions of people in your life, of situations, of events. Now repeat this modified form of Sentence 5 several times, each time inserting a different specific perception:

> He would release my mind from my perception of [name of a person], because it hides His face from me.
>
> He would release my mind from my perception of [this particular situation], because it hides His face from me.
>
> He would release my mind from my perception of [this specific event], because it hides His face from me.

5. Now let's try to apply the technique from Review III to Sentence 7. Read the sentence over:

> His strength is yours because He is the Self That God created as His only Son.

Place the sentence in your mind. Realize that it means, "Christ's strength is mine because He is my true Self." Silently repeat this form of it a couple of times. Let the meaning of it fill your mind.

Now lean back and let your mind creatively apply this truth to your needs, problems and concerns. Let these come to mind, one-by-one, and be answered as your mind applies to them this idea from the Course. You don't need to stick too close to this exact idea. If other Course-related understandings start coming to mind, let them come. Let your mind go where it wants to go with this.

If you get stuck, if no thoughts come for awhile, simply repeat Sentence 7 again once or twice, and then again let your mind creatively apply this idea to your current difficulties.

Did this work for you? Did it give you a different perspective on your needs, problems and concerns? If you were to do this regularly, do you think your life would be different?

Conclusion

In this book, we have hoped to show you that there are untold treasures awaiting us in the words of *A Course in Miracles*. To find those treasures and to experience their transformative benefits, each of us must mine them for ourselves. We hope we have succeeded in passing along some of the tools and techniques needed for this mining process.

Learning to use these techniques skillfully, easily, and as a matter of habit, will not happen overnight. Rather, it is perhaps a life-long process. You will probably go through starts and stops on this journey. There may well be long periods of time in which you get lazy and forget to apply these techniques. But you will probably start applying them once more when you remember how much more benefit you received when you used them.

As you begin to apply these techniques, don't try to use all of them at once. There are just too many. Instead, we have two suggestions. First, experiment. Try out the various techniques and find the ones that work best for you. You may discover, for instance, that you don't relate to following the logic, but that you do find great value in pinning down those pronouns.

Second, rather than trying to consciously apply all the techniques, just hold in mind the three basic categories: Observation, Interpretation, and Application:

- For Observation, have a mind-set of being highly aware of what you are reading. Try to notice everything. Ask yourself, "What does this *say*?"
- For Interpretation, hold in mind the goal of understanding the material. Be vigilant for when you don't understand, and be willing to go on a search for clarity. Ask yourself, "What does this *mean*?"
- For Application, have the desire to apply everything you read to your own life. Ask yourself, "What does this mean *to me and my life*?"

If you truly *want* to observe, interpret, and apply, you will naturally find yourself drawing on the specific techniques you have been taught in this book.

We also suggest that you return to this book from time to time in order to refresh yourself. You may want to read the whole thing over. You may simply want to brush up on one particular technique. In order to periodically refresh yourself, you may want to keep this book near where you keep your copy of the Course.

We end with quoting these words from Review III of the Workbook, which we believe can be applied to everything in the Text and Manual as well. May these words encourage you now, and in all your future study and application of the

Course:

> You have been given [these words] in perfect trust; in perfect confidence that you would use them well; in perfect faith that you would see their messages and use them for yourself. Offer them to your mind in that same trust and confidence and faith. It will not fail. It is the Holy Spirit's chosen means for your salvation. Since it has His trust, His means must surely merit yours as well. (W-pI.rIII.In.7:1–5)

the Circle of Atonement
Teaching & Healing Center

· *Publications* ·

· *Products* ·

· *Services* ·

based on **A Course in Miracles**

The Circle of Atonement
Teaching and Healing Center

is a non-profit, tax-exempt corporation founded in 1993, and is located in Sedona, Arizona. It is based on *A Course in Miracles*, the three-volume modern spiritual classic, which we believe was authored by Jesus through a human scribe.

A Note from the President

Dear Student:

Our conviction at The Circle of Atonement is that *A Course in Miracles* is a gold mine of spiritual wisdom, to be mined with the greatest care and respect. As we have attempted to do this, we believe we have found an answer to the perennial question of Course students, "How do I make it practical?" Our discovery is that the Course makes itself practical; that *A Course in Miracles* is a spiritual program laid out in detail, designed to lead us step-by-step to the lofty heights of which it speaks. If we simply follow its instructions, we will become happier, more loving and forgiving people, well on our way to complete liberation.

Our materials at the Circle are meant to help the student do just that: take the Course as a program. They are designed to aid the student in the study of the Text, the practice of the Workbook, and the fulfillment of one's function as a teacher of God. We offer these materials to you in the hope that they can serve you well on your journey home.

In Peace,

Robert Perry

P.S. We are committed to making our materials available to anyone regardless of their ability to pay. Please see our financial policy.

Mission Statement

To discern the author's vision of *A Course in Miracles* and manifest that in our lives, in the lives of students, and in the world.

1. To faithfully discern the author's vision of *A Course in Miracles*.

In interpreting the Course we strive for total fidelity to its words and the meanings they express. We thereby seek to discover the Course as the author saw it.

2. To be an instrument in Jesus' plan to manifest his vision of the Course in the lives of students and in the world.

We consider this to be Jesus' organization and therefore we attempt to follow his guidance in all we do. Our goal is to help students understand, as well as discern for themselves, the Course's thought system as he intended, and use it as he meant it to be used – as a literal program in spiritual awakening. Through doing so we hope to help ground in the world the intended way of doing the Course, here at the beginning of its history.

3. To help spark an enduring tradition based entirely on students joining together in doing the Course as the author envisioned.

We have a vision of local Course support systems composed of teachers, students, healers, and groups, all there to support one another in making full use of the Course. These support systems, as they continue and multiply, will together comprise an enduring spiritual tradition, dedicated solely to doing the Course as the author intended. Our goal is to help spark this tradition, and to assist others in doing the same.

4. To become an embodiment, a birthplace of this enduring spiritual tradition.

To help spark this tradition we must first become a model for it ourselves. This requires that we at the Circle follow the Course as our individual path; that we ourselves learn forgiveness through its program. It requires that we join with each other in a group holy relationship dedicated to the common goal of awakening through the Course. It also requires that we cultivate a local support system here in Sedona, and that we have a facility where others could join with us in learning this approach to the Course. Through all of this we hope to become a seed for an ongoing spiritual tradition based on *A Course in Miracles*.

Friends of the Circle
JOINING IN A COMMON VISION

If the vision of the Circle presented here speaks to you, we invite you to join with us in it. Ask yourself: Is this a vision I want to see promulgated in the world? Is this something I want to give my support to? If so, perhaps you would like to become a "Friend of the Circle." The benefits include:

Category 1: $60.00 per year*

- Four-issue subscription to our newsletter, *A Better Way*
- Updates and special reports every other month or so, making you an informed partner
- Support from one of our staff in your study and application of the Course
- Special materials and hand-outs on support groups, Text studies, responses to questions
- Feedback forms to give us your ideas and concerns
- Join us in our daily Workbook and meditation practice

Category 2: $130.00 per year* - Includes all of the above, plus
- Products and services, valued at a total of $70.00 (including appropriate shipping fees)

Quarterly payment plans are available for both categories, at a slightly higher cost.

*ALL PRICES ARE FOR U.S. ONLY, and are subject to change. Please contact The Circle of Atonement at (520) 282-0790 for the most current information.

TO BECOME A FRIEND OF THE CIRCLE

- Confirm the current price for the category membership you desire with the Circle.
- Write us a paragraph or two about why you want to become a Friend. What about this speaks to you?
- Take a few moments to silently join with us in purpose.
- Enclose your initial payment/donation (If you are unable to afford the amount listed, see our Financial Policy page 243).

Services Currently Offered

NEWSLETTER, BOOKS AND BOOKLETS - *A BETTER WAY* is the Circle's newsletter, published quarterly. It is primarily a teaching journal, containing articles by Robert, Allen and others, on the Course.

Our other publications, ranging in size from booklets to full-size books, are available in bookstores or directly from The Circle of Atonement. They are expositions of a theme or section from the Course.

THE LEARNING CIRCLE - This is our school for students of the Course, and is a division of the Teaching Wing. It is designed to aid students in their reading, study and understanding of the Course. The school, started in 1994, consists of introductory classes, Text study classes, and topical classes. Classes are available by correspondence following the in-person presentation of the class. Additional information is available by requesting our introductory packet (See Ordering Information, page 186.)

WORKSHOPS, SEMINARS AND RETREATS - The Circle currently offers workshops, seminars and retreats in Sedona. These are open to all individuals interested in *A Course in Miracles*. Dates and specifics are announced in every newsletter mailing (or call the Circle for more information and dates of events). Robert and Allen are available to speak at other locations by invitation.

SUPPORT SYSTEM - The Circle is currently developing a multi-faceted support system in Sedona, under the direction of Jeanne Cashin and Robert Perry. Currently in place are Support Meetings, designed to encourage sharing of how we apply Course principles to our lives, as well as Meditation Meetings, designed to facilitate the practice of the Lessons; one-on-one support for local students, as well as telephone support for students outside the local area. See Issue #18 of *A Better Way* for more information.

FINANCIAL POLICY

Our financial policy is based on a line in *Psychotherapy*, a supplement to *A Course in Miracles*: "One rule should always be observed: No one should be turned away because he cannot pay." Therefore, if you would like any of our materials or services and cannot afford them, simply let us know, and give what you are able.

The Circle is supported entirely by your purchases and gifts. Therefore, we ask you to look within to see if you might be led to support the Circle's vision financially with a donation above the list price of materials. We encourage you to give, not in payment for goods received, but in support of our present and future outreach. Please note that only amounts given over the list price are considered tax-deductible.

Please see *A Better Way*, Issue #18 for a more detailed explanation.

Our Teachers

Robert Perry brings to *A Course in Miracles* many years of private study and public teaching. He began teaching at Miracle Distribution Center in 1986, and has since then taught throughout North America and around the world. His teaching grows out of his dedication to the Course as his own path and his desire to assist others on this path. Over the years he has become a respected voice in Course circles and has written for many Course newsletters and magazines. Robert is the founder of The Circle of Atonement and the author of numerous books and booklets based on the Course, including the popular *An Introduction to "A Course in Miracles."*

Allen Watson is well known around the world to *A Course in Miracles* students for his helpful and insightful daily commentaries on the Workbook lessons which are on the Internet, as well as in book form, titled *A Workbook Companion, Volumes I, II and III*. Allen's gifted and spirited writing and teaching help students to unlock the meaning of *A Course in Miracles* for themselves. Allen is teaching a weekly class that is designed to cover the entire *A Course In Miracles* Text, section by section. His Text commentaries and Study Guides are also available through the Internet and will be published in a book series starting in 2000.

Books & Booklets

BASED ON *A COURSE IN MIRACLES*

An Introduction to *A Course in Miracles* – Perry; *A brief overview of the Course*; 44 pp.; **$2.95***

ACIM Interpretive Forum "Prosperity and *A Course in Miracles"* With Position Papers by Allen Watson and Tony Ponticello, and Response Papers by several participants, this journal seeks to explore the Course's position on material abundance and divine supply; 47 pp.; **$5.00***

The Elder Brother: Jesus in *A Course in Miracles* – Perry; *Jesus – the most celebrated man in history. We have prayed to him, loved him, feared him. But have we really known him?*

Perry examines the historical Jesus and compares him with the author of the Course. Was the Course authored by Jesus? Perry offers his own opinion as he lets the reader come to his or her own conclusion. Fascinating and inspiring reading for anyone interested in Jesus or the Course; 184 pp.; **$9.00***

 **#1 Seeing the Face of Christ in All Our Brothers** – Perry; *How we can see the Presence of God in others. This booklet seeks to present the Course's lofty vision of our Divine nature;* 47 pp.; **$5.00***

#3 Shrouded Vaults of the Mind – Perry; *Draws a map of the mind based on ACIM, and takes you on a tour through its many levels;* 44 pp.; **$5.00***

 **#4 Guidance: Living the Inspired Life** Perry; *Drawn from ACIM and Perry's own experience, this booklet sketches an overall perspective on guidance and its place on the spiritual path;* 44 pp.; **$5.00***

#6 Reality & Illusion: An Overview of Course Metaphysics Part I – Perry; *Examines the Course's vision of reality, attempting to answer the question: "What is real?";* 44 pp.; **$5.00***

 **#7 Reality & Illusion: An Overview of Course Metaphysics Part II** – Perry; *Examines questions such as: "Why are we here?" "How did we get here?" Discusses the origins of our apparent separation from God, and how to surmount the barriers to ultimate happiness;* 52 pp.; **$5.00***

 **#8 A Healed Mind Does Not Plan** Watson; *Examines our approach to planning and decision-making, showing how it is possible to leave the direction of our lives up to the Holy Spirit;* 40 pp.; **$5.00***

#9 Through Fear to Love – Watson; *Explores two sections from ACIM that deal with our fear of redemption and with the perception of the world that results from our fearful self-perception. It leads the reader to see how we can look on ourselves with love;* 44 pp.; **$5.00***

#10 The Journey Home Watson; *Sets forth a sequential description of the spiritual journey as seen in the Course. This booklet presents a map of sorts to give us an idea of our spiritual destination and what we must go through to get there;* 64 pp.; **$5.00***

#11 Everything You Always Wanted to Know About JUDGMENT But Were Too Busy Doing It to Notice  Perry & Watson; *A survey of various teachings about judgment in ACIM: What is judgment, giving up judgment, right use of judgment, judgment of the Holy Spirit, the Last Judgment;* 59 pp.; **$5.00***

Publications • Products • Services

#12 The Certainty of Salvation – Perry & Watson; *An antidote to feelings of discouragement, impatience, despair and doubt that may arise for those trying to reach the spiritual goal of the curriculum of the Course. Gathers together many of the Course's most encouraging and uplifting thoughts, reassuring us that attaining the goal is inevitable;* 51 pp.; **$5.00***

#13 What Is Death?
Watson; *Our belief in death is at the core of our painful experiences in this world. The author presents philosophical insights from the Course about the nature of death, and seeks to explain how to apply these principles in practical situations such as the death of a loved one, or facing death ourselves;* 42 pp.; **$5.00***

#14 The Workbook as a Spiritual Practice – Perry; *The Workbook of A Course in Miracles trains us in a profound new method of spiritual practice, and only through this practice will we realize the wonderful promises contained in the Course. This booklet is designed to help students get the most out of the Workbook, to help them find happiness through the training of their minds;* 57 pp.; **$5.00***

*ALL PRICES ARE FOR U.S. ONLY, and are subject to change. Please contact the Circle directly for the most current information.

#15 I Need Do Nothing: Finding the Quiet Center
Watson; *This phrase captures the heart of the Course's philosophy, yet it has also been the source of endless misunderstanding. This paragraph-by-paragraph commentary on the section, "I Need Do Nothing," seeks to draw out that heart as well as clear up the misunderstandings;* 57 pp.; **$5.00***

#16 A Course Glossary
Perry; *The Course employs a unique use of language in which it fills familiar terms with new meaning. This makes its language initially confusing, yet eventually transformative. This glossary attempts to clear up the confusion. Along with Course meanings, definitions include root, conventional, and Christian meanings. Intended for both new and experienced students, both individual and group study;* 96 pp.; perfect-bound; **$7.00***

#17 Seeing the Bible Differently: How *A Course in Miracles* Views the Bible
Watson; *Addresses the question, "How does the Course relate to the Bible?" Based on the Course's own attitude toward the Bible, it recognizes both similarities and differences, and emphasizes the continuity of God's message in the two books, seeing the Course as a clearer presentation of truth, which supersedes the Bible while standing clearly in its lineage;* 80 pp.; perfect-bound; **$6.00***

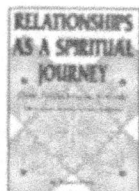

#18 Relationships as a Spiritual Journey: From Specialness to Holiness – Perry; *Describes the unique teaching of the Course on the subject of human relationships, that the quest for God is best accomplished in them. This requires, however, that our relationships go through profound transformation, from special relationships, based on the pursuit of individual specialness, to holy relationships, based on a truly common goal;* 192 pp.; perfect-bound; **$10.00***

A WORKBOOK COMPANION
Commentaries on the Workbook for Students from *A Course in Miracles*
by Allen Watson and Robert Perry

A three-volume set designed to aid students of the Course in their practice and understanding of the Workbook's daily lessons. Each volume includes a commentary and a practice summary of each lesson, as well as periodic overviews of the training goals of various lessons. These are not a replacement of the lessons themselves, but are rather a companion, with explanations, personal anecdotes, and advice on how to carry out the lessons. Each volume is perfect-bound.

#19	Volume I – covers Lessons 1 - 120	(320 pp.)	**$16.00***
#20	Volume II – covers Lessons 121 - 243	(304 pp.)	**$16.00***
#21	Volume III – covers Lessons 244 - 365	(352 pp.)	**$18.00***

Special Offer   ALL THREE VOLUMES - $45.00 (Reg. $50.00)

#22 The Answer is a Miracle
Perry and Watson; *A Course in Miracles promises to teach its students miracles, and who would not want to learn that? Yet the Course redefines miracles, causing many students to simply be confused about them. This book attempts to clear up that confusion and place miracles back where they belong, at the center of the Course, where we can learn them.;* 112 pp.; perfect bound; **$7.00***

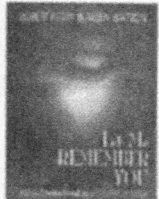

#23 Let Me Remember You: God in *A Course in Miracles*
Perry and Watson; *God is a central topic in human life and in A Course in Miracles. Little attention, however, has been given to God by most students and teachers of the Course. This book is an attempt to remedy that situation. It is designed to help readers gain, or perhaps, regain, a sense of God's relevance and immediacy.*
186 pp.; perfect bound; **$10.00***

#24 Bringing the Course to Life: How to Unlock the Meaning of *A Course in Miracles* for Yourself
Watson and Perry; *The words of* A Course in Miracles, *though beautiful and profound, are notoriously hard to understand. This book is designed to teach the student, through instruction, example, and exercises, how to read the Course. It is designed to transform the reading of the Course from a dry, frustrating experience into a living, personal encounter with truth;* 257 pp.; perfect-bound; **$12.00**

Source Material
FOR OUR PUBLICATIONS

The following four books are works that we encourage every student of the Course to own. By definition, a Course student owns the Course itself. But we also believe that the other three books below are highly valuable to one's journey with the Course. All of them contain additional material dictated by Jesus through Helen Schucman. For this reason, our writings draw on them frequently.

A Course in Miracles
(Hardcover)
$29.95*

The Gifts of God
This volume primarily contains Helen Schucman's poetry, which Helen felt she "received" from a deeper place in her own mind, not from the author of the Course. However, the volume closes with a fourteen-page piece, also called "The Gifts of God," which is not one of Helen's poems. Rather, it was perhaps Helen's final authentic scribing from Jesus. We, therefore, consider it part of the Course's "canon" and for that reason our publications sometimes quote from it. **$21.95***

Supplements to ACIM: Psychotherapy and Song of Prayer
These are two supplements to the Course, now together in one volume. They were dictated by the author of the Course to Helen Schucman after the Course's completion. The Circle's publications refer to both supplements often, as they are the same teaching as the Course from the same author. **$9.95***

Absence from Felicity, by Kenneth Wapnick. *This excellent "Story of Helen Schucman and Her Scribing of* A Course in Miracles" *has immense historical value for its telling of the story of the Course's birth. The reason that the Circle's writings often quote from it is that it also contains a great deal of personal guidance given by Jesus to Helen Schucman and Bill Thetford. It thus provides a window onto how Jesus envisioned the Course being applied in the everyday lives of two people.* **$16.00***

*ALL PRICES ARE FOR U.S. ONLY, and are subject to change. Please contact the Circle directly for the most current information.

The Vision of the Learning Circle

The Learning Circle is our school for students of *A Course in Miracles*. Our vision is to aid students in their personal study of the Course. Since the Course is a book, the foundational activity for any student is simply reading the book. This is doubly so for this particular course, for it makes the study and understanding of its thought system the foundation for walking its path. As the opening line of the Workbook says, "A theoretical foundation such as the text provides is necessary as a framework to make the exercises in this workbook meaningful."

Based on the above, that one reads the book, how one reads the book, and how much one understands its thought system are all crucial. All of these provide a foundation for giving meaning to the application of the Course. The purpose of The Learning Circle is to aid and support students in all of the above things:

~ *in reading the book*
~ *in reading it in a way that mines its treasures*
~ *in understanding what it says*
~ *in seeing how this understanding applies in our lives*

Our experience has been that this reading, study and understanding are indeed the foundation for the entire path of the Course. As students become more firmly grounded in this, their experience of the Course and their ability to apply it increase exponentially.

The Correspondence School

If you are unable to attend the classes offered in person, and wish to participate in The Learning Circle program, the tape sets from the classes are available as correspondence classes. Each correspondence class consists of a reading list, a study guide, student feedback forms, and student-teacher interaction via phone, e-mail, tape recording and/or writing. At the completion of a correspondence class, the student receives a certificate of completion from The Learning Circle.

Two of our correspondence class tape sets, 101 and 102, serve as prerequisites for continuing study with The Learning Circle, either through correspondence classes or in-person seminars. For more information, please request our information packet, which outlines the school program and class offerings (see Ordering Information, page 257).

The Learning Circle

TAPE SETS

The unedited live classes given in Sedona for students participating in our school are available on audio tape. If you are simply interested in listening to the classes, but not participating in the school, you may order the tape sets (and study guides, if desired), which are described below. If you would like to participate in the Correspondence School, receiving feedback from the teachers, please request first The Learning Circle brochure on the Ordering Form, page 257.

Study Guides $10.00
Study guides are available for use with all tape sets except 101. Each study guide can be used alone or in connection with its corresponding tape set. All study guides are $10.00 each. When ordering, please be sure to specify the tape set number for which you want a study guide.

101 Basic Introduction to
A Course in Miracles – Watson
Six 60-min. tapes $30.00
For familiarizing students with the perspective of the Circle's instructors; offers an overview of the Course's message and thought system; the Course as a spiritual path; and more.

102 Bringing the Course to Life: Turning Study Into Experience
Perry and Watson
Eight 90-min. tapes $40.00
An intensive focusing on methods and techniques for studying the Course, taking into consideration its unique presentation of its thought system.

Text Study Series
A detailed paragraph-by-paragraph study of the chapters specified.

201 Text Study, Chapters 1 - 3
Watson
Ten 90-minute tapes $50.00
1: The Meaning of Miracles
2: The Separation and the Atonement
3: The Innocent Perception

202 Text Study, Chapters 4 - 6
Perry & Watson
Ten 90-minute tapes $50.00
4: The Illusions of the Ego
5: Healing and Wholeness
6: The Lessons of Love

203 Text Study, Chapters 7 - 8
Perry & Watson
Ten 90-minute tapes $50.00
7: The Gifts of the Kingdom
8: The Journey Back

204 Text Study, Chapters 9 - 11
Perry & Watson
Ten 90-minute tapes $50.00
9: The Acceptance of the Atonement
10: The Idols of Sickness
11: God or the Ego

205 Text Study, Chapters 12 - 13
Perry & Watson
Ten 90-minute tapes $50.00
12: The Holy Spirit's Curriculum
13: The Guiltless World

206 Text Study, Chapters 14 - 15
Perry & Watson
Ten 90-minute tapes $50.00
14: Teaching for Truth
15: The Holy Instant

207 Text Study, Chapters 16 - 17
Perry & Watson
Ten 90-minute tapes $50.00
16: The Forgiveness of Illusions
17: Forgiveness and The Holy Relationship

The Learning Circle

208 Text Study, Chapters 18 - 19
Perry & Watson
Twelve 90-minute tapes $50.00
18: The Passing of The Dream
19: The Attainment of Peace

209 Text Study, Chapters 20 - 21
Perry & Watson
Ten 90-minute tapes $50.00
20: The Vision of Holiness
21: Reason and Perception

210 Text Study, Chapters 22 - 24
Perry & Watson
Twelve 90-minute tapes $50.00
22: Salvation and The Holy Relationship
23: The War Against Yourself
24: The Goal of Specialness

211 Text Study, Chapters 25 - 26
Perry & Watson
Eleven 90-minute tapes $50.00
25: The Justice of God
26: The Transition

212 Text Study, Chapters 27 - 28
Perry & Watson
Eleven 90-minute tapes $50.00
27: The Healing of The Dream
28: The Undoing of Fear

213 Text Study, Chapters 29 - 30
Perry & Watson
Eleven 90-minute tapes $50.00
29: The Awakening
30: The New Beginning

214 Text Study, Chapter 31
Perry & Watson
Ten 90-minute tapes $50.00
31: The Final Vision

Topical Study Series
Each tape set focuses on a particular theme derived from the Course, determined to be of interest or a keynote for understanding.

301 Perception and Vision
Perry
Ten 90-minute tapes $ 50.00
Includes: Projection makes perception; true perception and vision; dream roles and shadow figures; Holy Spirit's interpretation; eyes of the body and eyes of Christ.

302 The Holy Instant
Perry & Watson
Ten 90-minute tapes $ 50.00
Includes a focus on chapter 15 of the Text.

303 Judgment
Perry & Watson
Ten 90-minute tapes $ 50.00
Includes study of what judgment really is; how the Holy Spirit uses judgment; how we can release it; and more.

304 The Certainty of Salvation
Perry & Watson
Ten 90-minute tapes $ 50.00
Includes the what's, why's, and how's of salvation; our nature and the journey; God's changelessness; the happy learner; who walks with us?

305 We Are the Light of the World
Perry & Watson
Ten 90-minute tapes $50.00
An exploration of our function in this world as givers of forgiveness and healing. Includes: our special function, extension, our function is our happiness.

---

*ALL PRICES ARE FOR U.S. ONLY, and are subject to change. Please contact the Circle directly for the most current information.

The Learning Circle

306 Holy Relationships
Perry & Watson
Ten 90-minute tapes $50.00
Covers this important and controversial topic in the Course, carefully defining what the Course means by holy relationships, how they begin, progress and reach their goal.

307 Forgiveness
Perry & Watson
Ten 90-minute tapes $50.00
The theory and practice of forgiveness; how the Course defines forgiveness contrasted with what the word means in our culture; forgiveness practices.

308 God
Perry & Watson
Ten 90-minute tapes $50.00
A comprehensive treatment of this central, but under-appreciated topic in the Course. What God is; our fear of God; what God knows about our earthly lives; God's relationship with the Holy Spirit; prayer.

309 A Course in *What*?
Perry & Watson
Ten 90-minute tapes $50.00
Topics include: What is a miracle? Are miracles internal or interpersonal? Do they heal bodies? What is a miracle worker? How is the Course a course *in* miracles?

310 Time
Perry & Watson
Ten 90-minute tapes $50.00
Includes eternity and the unreality of time; the ego's repetition of the past; entering the present moment; saving time; patience.

311 The Body
Perry & Watson
Ten 90-minute tapes $50.00
Everything about the body: pleasure, pain, appearance, attractiveness, sex, the senses, the body's neutrality, its origin, the Holy Spirit's use of the body.

312 The Holy Spirit at Work in Our Lives
Perry & Watson
Ten 90-minute tapes $50.00
Primarily focuses on the role of receiving guidance from the Holy Spirit, including how to hear Him, the daily practice of asking, resistance to hearing, discernment of what is heard.

313 Sickness and Healing
Perry & Watson
Ten 90-minute tapes $50.00
Why we get sick; how to view illnesses in ourselves and others; finding healing for ourselves; giving healing to others; our calling as healers of patients.

"Bill has very intelligently suggested that you both should set yourself the goal of really studying for this course. There can be no doubt of the wisdom of this decision, for any student who wants to pass it." (Message given to Helen Schucman, scribe of *A Course in Miracles*; found in *Absence from Felicity*, p. 285)

Manual Study Series

Study of the *Manual for Teachers*
Robert Perry

This class attempts to mine the rich teaching in the Manual for Teachers. In addition to the usual detailed paragraph-by-paragraph study of the specified sections, the class tries to discern and internalize the Manual's instructions to us as teachers of God (even though the term may only partially apply to us). As a manual for own lives, what does it have to tell us about how to live our lives, walk our path, and carry out our function?

501: Introduction through Section 8	$50.00
502 : Sections 9 through 23	$50.00
503: Sections 24 through Epilogue	$50.00
Study guides for each tape set	$10.00

Study guides will be available in book form in Fall 1999.

Special Offer:
All 3 tape sets $125.00 (Reg. $150)

Announcing Our Electronic Text Class

The Electronic Text Class (ETC) is a new E-mail series of combined commentaries and study guides on the Text of *A Course in Miracles*, written by Allen Watson. Allen's Internet Workbook commentaries have generated such enthusiastic feedback that we decided to do something similar for the Text. These commentaries provide a bridge into the world of the Text. They help you to understand its message, appreciate its wonders, and see its relevance to your life; and they provide study tools to help you understand the Course on your own. They are designed for use by groups as well as individuals.

ETC commentary schedule and format:

The Text commentaries will be E-mailed weekly, with three 13-week trimesters every year. The expected duration of the on-line series is seven years. Commentaries will be compiled into book form beginning January 2000.

Each commentary will cover no more than one section of the Text, and will include the following features:

- informal commentary for each paragraph of the Text
- study question(s) for each paragraph (with Answer Key)
- study notes
- suggested exercises

For more information and assitance in subscribing on-line, please direct your web browser to: http://nen.sedona.net/circleofa/news-etc.html

Subscription Cost:

1999 first trimester (6 wks) back issues	$10.00
1999 2-1/2 trimesters	$42.00
Single trimester	$20.00
3 consecutive trimesters	$50.00

How to Subscribe:

For more information please request our information packet (see Ordering Information, page 257). Or you can order by E-mail (using credit card *only*).

Subscription E-mail should be sent to: circleofa@sedona.net. *Please be sure to clearly print your E-mail address and your regular mailing address on your subscription request.*

BACK NEWSLETTER ISSUES OF
A Better Way

Back issues of A Better Way newsletter are available for $2.00 per copy and Special Christmas Letter for $.50 each. Bolded titles are the lead articles in each issue. All articles by Robert Perry, unless otherwise noted.

Vol. 1, No. 1   Oct. 1991
The Ocean and the Grain of Sand
- How This Booklet Series and Newsletter Came About
- Summary and Commentary on Workbook Lesson 61

Vol. 2, No. 1   Jan. 1992
A Parable of Special Relationships
- Enlightenment is a Recognition
- Summary and Commentary on "The Choice for Completion"

Vol. 2, No. 2   Apr. 1992
Are We Responsible?
- Healing and *A Course in Miracles*, Judy Allen
- Summary and Commentary on "I Need Do Nothing"

Vol. 2, No. 3   June 1992
The Course and Other Paths
- How I Found the Course, Mary Eagle
- Summary and Commentary on "The Sole Responsibility of the Miracle Worker"

Vol. 2, No. 4   Oct. 1992
The Beginnings of a Center
- The Holy Hundredth of an Instant, Don Giacobbe
- How I Found the Course, Bernard Lacroix
- Summary and Commentary on "The Circle of Atonement"

Vol. 3, No. 1   Jan. 1993
The Course and Mother Nature
- My Little Guru

Vol. 3, No. 2   June 1993
The Course and the Intellect
- ACIM Interpretive Forum
- Our Attitude Towards Other Teachers, Allen Watson

Vol. 3, No. 3   Oct. 1993
What Is the Manual for Teachers?
- Allen Watson to Join the Circle
- How I Found the Course, Ron Johnson
- Idols As Defined by the Course

Vol. 4, No. 1   Apr. 1994
The Spiritual Path of A Course in Miracles
- ACIM Support System
- The Learning Circle

Vol. 4, No. 3   Sept. 1994
Willingness to Practice Every Step, Allen Watson
- Individual Responsibility and Interpersonal Relationship
- Meditation in the Course

Vol. 4, No. 4   Dec. 1994
Special Christmas Letter
- Christmas: The Birth of Holiness Into This World
- We Celebrate Christmas By Repeating It

Vol. 5, No. 1   Feb. 1995
How Long Until I Am Out of Here?
- The Practice of Mental Vigilance, Allen Watson
- Book reviews by Allen Watson: Love Always Answers, Diane Berke Awaken to Your Own Call, Jon Mundy

A Better Way

Vol. 5, No. 2   July 1995
Three Aspects of Our Relationship with God
- Receiving the Holy Instant, *Allen Watson*
- Stages of Practice, *Allen Watson*
- A Brief Summary of *A Course in Miracles*

Vol. 5, No. 3   Oct. 1995
The Teacher-Pupil Relationship: Does the Manual for Teachers Describe It?
- Sacred Tenets of the Special Relationship
- A Case of Mistaken Identity, *Allen Watson*
- The Six Rules of What is Wrong in Our Relationship

Vol. 5, No. 4   Dec. 1996
Special Christmas Letter
- The Advent of *A Course in Miracles*
- Be Born in Us Today, *Allen Watson*

Vol. 6, No. 1   Feb. 1996
The Importance of Relationships, Allen Watson
- The Form and Content of Being a Teacher
- How Do We Find a Teacher?: A Commentary on "Who Are Their Pupils?"

Vol. 6, No. 2   May 1996
Here I Am, Lord
- How Jesus Helps, *Allen Watson*
- An Editorial on Jesus Channeling
- What Exactly Does a Personal Teacher Do?
- "Who Walks With Me," a song by *Allen Watson*

Vol. 6, No. 3   Aug. 1996
There Is No Salvation in Form
- How Jesus Applied the Course to the Lives of Helen and Bill
- Handling Our Fears, *Allen Watson*
- His Recognition of Us
- Loving, Our Sacred Trust, *Allen Watson*

Vol. 6, No. 4   Dec. 1996
Who Wrote A Course in Miracles? Part I
- My Journey With the Workbook
- Jesus Reborn in Us, *Allen Watson* (Christmas Message)
- Healing and *A Course in Miracles:* On Becoming a Course "Healer-in-Training," *Thomas Dunn*

Issue #18   Apr. 1997
How Can A Course in Miracles Accomplish Its Purpose? Our Vision for The Circle of Atonement
- Traditional Monastic Pursuit in the Context of Contemporary Society
- We Go Together, You and I, *Jeanne Cashin*

Issue #19   July 1997
Who Wrote A Course in Miracles? Part II
- 12 Remedies for the Wandering Mind
- Bringing the Course to Life, Part 1, *Allen Watson*

Issue #20   Nov. 1997
"Be In My Mind, My Father": An Appreciation of the Prayer for Lesson 232
- Bringing the Course to Life, Part 2, *Allen Watson*
- Welcome Me Not Into a Manger (Christmas Message)
- Seeing the Meaning in the Idea for the Day
- Tips on Practice: Reading Aloud and Expanded Prayers, *Allen Watson*
- Tips for Study Groups: Using the Text Studies Tapes, *Allen Watson*
- Psychotherapy and *A Course in Miracles*, *Thomas Dunn*

A Better Way

Issue #21   Feb. 1998
Does God Know We Are Here?
- Bringing the Course to Life, Part 3, *Allen Watson*
- Being Truly Helpful
- Frequently Asked Questions: How can we distinguish between the ego and the Holy Spirit?, *Allen Watson*
- True Prayer

Issue #22   May 1998
The Course on Childhood
- Class 102, Bringing the Course to Life
- Bringing the Course to Life, Part 4, *Allen Watson*
- Misunderstood Passages: Trust Not Your Good Intentions, *Allen Watson*
- How Holy is the Smallest Grain of Sand!
- Let Me Behold My Savior

Issue #23   Aug. 1998
Course-Based Parenting, Part I
- Bringing the Course to Life, Part 5, *Allen Watson*
- Hearing God's Voice Means Joining, *Allen Watson*
- All My Sorrows End in Your Embrace
- A Self-Study Course?

Issue #24   Dec. 1998
How Do We Forgive?
- Bringing the Course to Life, Part 6, *Allen Watson*
- Course-Based Parenting, Part II
- Difficult Passages: Think Not You Made the World?
- The Birth of Holiness into this World (Christmas Message)

Issue #25   March 1999
This Is As Every Day Should Be
- Does Behavior Matter?, *Greg Mackie*
- Bringing the Course to Life, Part 7, *Allen Watson*

Issue #26   May 1999
If A Brother Asks You For Something Outrageous
- Gentle Firmness, *Greg Mackie*
- Bringing the Course to Life, Part 8, *Allen Watson*
- Big Daddy or Divine Desert?

Issue #27   August 1999
What Is "A Course in Miracles?"
- An Open Letter to Ken Wapnick
- Appreciating the Masterpiece, Part 1, *Greg Mackie*
- Artistic Techniques Used in the Course, *Greg Mackie*

A list of *Reprinted Articles* by Allen Watson and Robert Perry from other Course-based publications is available upon request. Please mark your interest on the Ordering Information Form on page 257.

Subscriptions for *A Better Way* Newsletter

A Better Way is designed as a teaching journal for students of the Course. The suggested subscription price is $10. U.S. in the U.S., $14. U.S. in Canada/Mexico, and $18. U.S. in all other countries, for four quarterly issues. *See Ordering Information Form on pg. 257*

Ordering Information

All publications and products listed previously are available as of this printing. ALL PRICES ARE FOR U.S. ONLY, and are subject to change. In addition, new titles become available regularly; therefore, please contact the Circle directly for the most current information.

Information is available by writing or calling us at:

The Circle of Atonement
Teaching and Healing Center

P.O. Box 4238 • W. Sedona, AZ 86340
Phone: (520) 282-0790 • Fax: (520) 282-0523
In the U.S. toll-free: (888) 357-7520 (for orders only)
e-mail: circleofa@sedona.net

Or

You can learn more and order materials directly from our website at
http://nen.sedona.net/circleofa/

Or

You can send the form below to the above address
with your information:

NAME _____

ADDRESS _____

CITY _____ PROVINCE/STATE _____

COUNTRY _____ POSTAL/ZIP CODE _____

PHONE _____

☐ Please send me a packet including information on current products, newsletter subscriptions, The Learning Circle Program, and Friends of the Circle membership

☐ Please send me a free list of reprinted articles

BCL-24

www.ingramcontent.com/pod-product-compliance
Lightning Source LLC
Chambersburg PA
CBHW022355040426
42450CB00005B/185